P9-DOF-629

THE PELICAN SHAKESPEARE
GENERAL EDITORS

STEPHEN ORGEL
A. R. BRAUNMULLER

The Tempest

Sir Herbert Beerbohm Tree as Caliban, 1904
(Drawing by Charles A. Buchel, *The Tatler*)

William Shakespeare

The Tempest

EDITED BY PETER HOLLAND

PENGUIN BOOKS

PENGUIN BOOKS

Published by the Penguin Group

Penguin Group (USA) Inc., 375 Hudson Street, New York, New York 10014, U.S.A.
Penguin Group (Canada), 90 Eglinton Avenue East, Suite 700, Toronto, Ontario,
Canada M4P 2Y3 (a division of Pearson Penguin Canada Inc.)
Penguin Books Ltd, 80 Strand, London WC2R 0RL, England
Penguin Ireland, 25 St Stephen's Green, Dublin 2, Ireland
(a division of Penguin Books Ltd)
Penguin Group (Australia), 250 Camberwell Road, Camberwell, Victoria 3124, Australia
(a division of Pearson Australia Group Pty Ltd)
Penguin Books India Pvt Ltd, 11 Community Centre, Panchsheel Park,
New Delhi – 110 017, India
Penguin Group (NZ), 67 Apollo Drive, Rosedale, North Shore 0632, New Zealand
(a division of Pearson New Zealand Ltd)
Penguin Books (South Africa) (Pty) Ltd, 24 Sturdee Avenue, Rosebank,
Johannesburg 2196, South Africa

Penguin Books Ltd, Registered Offices: 80 Strand, London WC2R 0RL, England

The Tempest edited by Northrop Frye published in the United
States of America in Penguin Books 1959
Revised edition published 1970
This new edition edited by Peter Holland published 1999

21 23 25 27 29 30 28 26 24 22

Copyright © Penguin Books Inc., 1959, 1970
Copyright © Penguin Putnam Inc., 1999
All rights reserved

ISBN 978-0-14-071485-2

Printed in the United States of America
Set in Garamond
Designed by Virginia Norey

Except in the United States of America, this book is sold subject to the condition
that it shall not, by way of trade or otherwise, be lent, resold, hired out, or otherwise
circulated without the publisher's prior consent in any form of binding or cover other
than that in which it is published and without a similar condition including
this condition being imposed on the subsequent purchaser.

The scanning, uploading and distribution of this book via the Internet or via any
other means without the permission of the publisher is illegal and punishable by law.
Please purchase only authorized electronic editions, and do not participate in or encourage
electronic piracy of copyrighted materials. Your support of the author's rights is appreciated.

Contents

Publisher's Note

IT IS ALMOST half a century since the first volumes of the Pelican Shakespeare appeared under the general editorship of Alfred Harbage. The fact that a new edition, rather than simply a revision, has been undertaken reflects the profound changes textual and critical studies of Shakespeare have undergone in the past twenty years. For the new Pelican series, the texts of the plays and poems have been thoroughly revised in accordance with recent scholarship, and in some cases have been entirely reedited. New introductions and notes have been provided in all the volumes. But the new Shakespeare is also designed as a successor to the original series; the previous editions have been taken into account, and the advice of the previous editors has been solicited where it was feasible to do so.

Certain textual features of the new Pelican Shakespeare should be particularly noted. All lines are numbered that contain a word, phrase, or allusion explained in the glossarial notes. In addition, for convenience, every tenth line is also numbered, in italics when no annotation is indicated. The intrusive and often inaccurate place headings inserted by early editors are omitted (as is becoming standard practice), but for the convenience of those who miss them, an indication of locale now appears as the first item in the annotation of each scene.

In the interest of both elegance and utility, each speech prefix is set in a separate line when the speaker's lines are in verse, except when those words form the second half of a verse line. Thus the verse form of the speech is kept visually intact. What is printed as verse and what is printed as prose has, in general, the authority of the original texts. Departures from the original texts in this regard have only the authority of editorial tradition and the judgment of the Pelican editors; and, in a few instances, are admittedly arbitrary.

The Theatrical World

Economic realities determined the theatrical world in which Shakespeare's plays were written, performed, and received. For centuries in England, the primary theatrical tradition was nonprofessional. Craft guilds (or "mysteries") provided religious drama – mystery plays – as part of the celebration of religious and civic festivals, and schools and universities staged classical and neoclassical drama in both Latin and English as part of their curricula. In these forms, drama was established and socially acceptable. Professional theater, in contrast, existed on the margins of society. The acting companies were itinerant; playhouses could be any available space – the great halls of the aristocracy, town squares, civic halls, inn yards, fair booths, or open fields – and income was sporadic, dependent on the passing of the hat or on the bounty of local patrons. The actors, moreover, were considered little better than vagabonds, constantly in danger of arrest or expulsion.

In the late 1560s and 1570s, however, English professional theater began to gain respectability. Wealthy aristocrats fond of drama – the Lord Admiral, for example, or the Lord Chamberlain – took acting companies under their protection so that the players technically became members of their households and were no longer subject to arrest as homeless or masterless men. Permanent theaters were first built at this time as well, allowing the companies to control and charge for entry to their performances.

Shakespeare's livelihood, and the stunning artistic explosion in which he participated, depended on pragmatic and architectural effort. Professional theater requires ways to restrict access to its offerings; if it does not, and admission fees cannot be charged, the actors do not get paid, the costumes go to a pawnbroker, and there is no such thing as a professional, ongoing theatrical tradition. The answer to that economic need arrived in the late 1560s and 1570s with the creation of the so-called public or amphitheater playhouse. Recent discoveries indicate that the precursor of the Globe playhouse in London (where Shakespeare's mature plays were presented) and the Rose theater (which presented Christopher Marlowe's plays and some of Shakespeare's earliest ones) was the Red Lion theater of 1567. Archaeological studies of the foundations of the Rose and Globe theaters have revealed that the open-air theater of the 1590s and later was probably a polygonal building with fourteen to twenty or twenty-four sides, multistoried, from 75 to 100 feet in diameter, with a raised, partly covered "thrust" stage that projected into a group of standing patrons, or "groundlings," and a covered gallery, seating up to 2,500 or more (very crowded) spectators.

These theaters might have been about half full on any given day, though the audiences were larger on holidays or when a play was advertised, as old and new were, through printed playbills posted around London. The metropolitan area's late-Tudor, early-Stuart population (circa 1590-1620) has been estimated at about 150,000 to 250,000. It has been supposed that in the mid-1590s there were about 15,000 spectators per week at the public theaters; thus, as many as 10 percent of the local population went to the theater regularly. Consequently, the theaters' repertories – the plays available for this experienced and frequent audience – had to change often: in the month between September 15 and October 15, 1595, for instance, the Lord Admiral's Men performed twenty-eight times in eighteen different plays.

Since natural light illuminated the amphitheaters' stages, performances began between noon and two o'clock and ran without a break for two or three hours. They often concluded with a jig, a fencing display, or some other nondramatic exhibition. Weather conditions determined the season for the amphitheaters: plays were performed every day (including Sundays, sometimes, to clerical dismay) except during Lent – the forty days before Easter – or periods of plague, or sometimes during the summer months when law courts were not in session and the most affluent members of the audience were not in London.

To a modern theatergoer, an amphitheater stage like that of the Rose or Globe would appear an unfamiliar mixture of plainness and elaborate decoration. Much of the structure was carved or painted, sometimes to imitate marble; elsewhere, as under the canopy projecting over the stage, to represent the stars and the zodiac. Appropriate painted canvas pictures (of Jerusalem, for example, if the play was set in that city) were apparently hung on the wall behind the acting area, and tragedies were accompanied by black hangings, presumably something like crepe festoons or bunting. Although these theaters did not employ what we would call scenery, early modern spectators saw numerous large props, such as the "bar" at which a prisoner stood during a trial, the "mossy bank" where lovers reclined, an arbor for amorous conversation, a chariot, gallows, tables, trees, beds, thrones, writing desks, and so forth. Audiences might learn a scene's location from a sign (reading "Athens," for example) carried across the stage (as in Bertolt Brecht's twentieth-century productions). Equally captivating (and equally irritating to the theater's enemies) were the rich costumes and personal props the actors used: the most valuable items in the surviving theatrical inventories are the swords, gowns, robes, crowns, and other items worn or carried by the performers.

Magic appealed to Shakespeare's audiences as much as it does to us today, and the theater exploited many deceptive and spectacular devices. A winch in the loft above the stage, called "the heavens," could lower and raise actors playing gods, goddesses, and other supernatural figures to and from the main acting area, just as one or more trapdoors permitted entrances and exits to and from the area, called "hell," beneath the stage. Actors wore elementary makeup such as wigs, false beards, and face paint, and they employed pig's bladders filled with animal blood to make wounds seem more real. They had rudimentary but effective ways of pretending to behead or hang a person. Supernumeraries (stagehands or actors not needed in a particular scene) could make thunder sounds (by shaking a metal sheet or rolling an iron ball down a chute) and show lightning (by blowing inflammable resin through tubes into a flame). Elaborate fireworks enhanced the effects of dragons flying through the air or imitated such celestial phenomena as comets, shooting stars, and multiple suns. Horses' hoofbeats, bells (located perhaps in the tower above the stage), trumpets and drums, clocks, cannon shots and gunshots, and the like were common sound effects. And the music of viols, cornets, oboes, and recorders was a regular feature of theatrical performances.

For two relatively brief spans, from the late 1570s to 1590 and from 1599 to 1614, the amphitheaters competed with the so-called private, or indoor, theaters, which originated as, or later represented themselves as, educational institutions training boys as singers for church services and court performances. These indoor theaters had two features that were distinct from the amphitheaters': their personnel and their playing spaces. The amphitheaters' adult companies included both adult men, who played the male roles, and boys, who played the female roles; the private, or indoor, theater companies, on the other hand, were entirely composed of boys aged about 8 to 16, who were, or could pretend to be, candidates for singers in a church or a royal boys' choir. (Until 1660, professional theatrical companies included no women.) The playing space would appear much more familiar to modern audiences than the long-vanished amphitheaters; the later indoor theaters were, in fact, the ancestors of the typical modern theater. They were enclosed spaces, usually rectangular, with the stage filling one end of the rectangle and the audience arrayed in seats or benches across (and sometimes lining) the building's longer axis. These spaces staged plays less frequently than the public theaters (perhaps only once a week) and held far fewer spectators than the amphitheaters: about 200 to 600, as opposed to 2,500 or more. Fewer patrons mean a smaller gross income, unless each pays more. Not surprisingly, then, private theaters charged higher prices than the amphitheaters, probably sixpence, as opposed to a penny for the cheapest entry.

Protected from the weather, the indoor theaters presented plays later in the day than the amphitheaters, and used artificial illumination – candles in sconces or candelabra. But candles melt, and need replacing, snuffing, and trimming, and these practical requirements may have been part of the reason the indoor theaters introduced breaks in the performance, the intermission so dear to the heart of theatergoers and to the pocketbooks of theater concessionaires ever since. Whether motivated by the need to tend to the candles or by the entrepreneurs' wishing to sell oranges and liquor, or both, the indoor theaters eventually established the modern convention of the non-continuous performance. In the early modern "private" theater, musical performances apparently filled the intermissions, which in Stuart theater jargon seem to have been called "acts."

At the end of the first decade of the seventeenth century, the distinction between public amphitheaters and private indoor companies ceased. For various cultural, political, and economic reasons, individual companies gained control of both the public, open-air theaters and the indoor ones, and companies mixing adult men and boys took over the formerly "private" theaters. Despite the death of the boys' companies and of their highly innovative theaters (for which such luminous playwrights as Ben Jonson, George Chapman, and John Marston wrote), their playing spaces and conventions had an immense impact on subsequent plays: not merely for the intervals (which stressed the artistic and architectonic importance of "acts"), but also because they introduced political and social satire as a popular dramatic ingredient, even in tragedy, and a wider range of actorly effects, encouraged by their more intimate playing spaces.

Even the briefest sketch of the Shakespearean theatrical world would be incomplete without some comment on the social and cultural dimensions of theaters and playing in the period. In an intensely hierarchical and status-conscious society, professional actors and their ventures had hardly any respectability; as we have indicated, to protect themselves against laws designed to curb vagabondage and the increase of masterless men, actors resorted to the near-fiction that they were the servants of noble masters, and wore their distinctive livery. Hence the company for which Shakespeare wrote in the 1590s called itself the Lord Chamberlain's Men and pretended that the public, money-getting performances were in fact rehearsals for private per-formances before that high court official. From 1598, the Privy Council had licensed theatrical companies, and after 1603, with the accession of King James I, the companies gained explicit royal protection, just as the Queen's Men had for a time under Queen Elizabeth. The Chamberlain's Men became the King's Men, and the other companies were patronized by the other members of the royal family.

These designations were legal fictions that half-concealed an important economic and social develop-ment, the evolution away from the theater's organization on the model of the guild, a self-regulating confraternity of individual artisans, into a proto-capitalist organization. Shakespeare's company became a joint-stock company, where persons who supplied capital and, in some cases, such as Shakespeare's, capital and talent, employed them-selves and others in earning a return on that capital. This development meant that actors and theater companies were outside both the traditional guild structures, which required some form of civic or royal charter, and the feu-dal household organization of master-and-servant. This anomalous, maverick social and economic condition made theater companies practically unruly and potentially even dangerous; consequently, numerous official bodies – including the London metropolitan and ecclesiastical authorities as well as, occasionally, the royal court itself – tried, without much success, to control and even to disband them.

Public officials had good reason to want to close the theaters: they were attractive nuisances – they drew often riotous crowds, they were always noisy, and they could be politically offensive and socially insubordinate. Until the Civil War, however, anti-theatrical forces failed to shut down professional theater, for many reasons – limited surveillance and few police powers, tensions or outright hostilities among the agencies that sought to check or channel theatrical activity, and lack of clear policies for control. Another reason must have been the theaters' undeniable popularity. Curtailing any activity enjoyed by such a substantial percentage of the population was difficult, as various Roman emperors attempting to limit circuses had learned, and the Tudor-Stuart audience was not merely large, it was socially diverse and included women. The prevalence of public entertainment in this period has been underestimated. In fact, fairs, holidays, games, sporting events, the equivalent of modern parades, freak shows, and street exhibitions all abounded, but the theater was the most widely and frequently available entertainment to which people of every class had access. That fact helps account both for its quantity and for the fear and anger it aroused.

WILLIAM SHAKESPEARE OF
STRATFORD-UPON-AVON, GENTLEMAN

Many people have said that we know very little about William Shakespeare's life – pinheads and postcards are often mentioned as appropriately tiny surfaces on which to record the available information. More imaginatively and perhaps more correctly, Ralph Waldo Emerson wrote, "Shakespeare is the only biographer of Shakespeare. . . . So far from Shakespeare's being the least known, he is the one person in all modern history fully known to us."

In fact, we know more about Shakespeare's life than we do about almost any other English writer's of his era. His last will and testament (dated March 25, 1616) survives, as do numerous legal contracts and court documents involving Shakespeare as principal or witness, and parish records in Stratford and London. Shakespeare appears quite often in official records of King James's royal court, and of course Shakespeare's name appears on numerous title pages and in the written and recorded words of his literary contemporaries Robert Greene, Henry Chettle, Francis Meres, John Davies of Hereford, Ben Jonson, and many others. Indeed, if we make due allowance for the bloating of modern, run-of-the-mill bureaucratic records, more information has survived over the past four hundred years about William Shakespeare of Stratford-upon-Avon, Warwickshire, than is likely to survive in the next four hundred years about any reader of these words.

What we do not have are entire categories of information – Shakespeare's private letters or diaries, drafts and revisions of poems and plays, critical prefaces or essays, commendatory verse for other writers' works, or instructions guiding his fellow actors in their performances, for instance – that we imagine would help us understand and appreciate his surviving writings. For all we know, many such data never existed as written records. Many literary and theatrical critics, not knowing what might once have existed, more or less cheerfully accept the situation; some even make a theoretical virtue of it by claiming that such data are irrelevant to understanding and interpreting the plays and poems.

So, what do we know about William Shakespeare, the man responsible for thirty-seven or perhaps more plays, more than 150 sonnets, two lengthy narrative poems, and some shorter poems?

While many families by the name of Shakespeare (or some variant spelling) can be identified in the English Midlands as far back as the twelfth century, it seems likely that the dramatist's grandfather, Richard, moved to Snitterfield, a town not far from Stratford-upon-Avon, sometime before 1529. In Snitterfield, Richard Shakespeare leased farmland from the very wealthy Robert Arden. By 1552, Richard's son John had moved to a large house on Henley Street in Stratford-upon-Avon, the house that stands today as "The Birthplace." In Stratford, John Shakespeare traded as a glover, dealt in wool, and lent money at interest; he also served in a variety of civic posts, including "High Bailiff," the municipality's equivalent of mayor. In 1557, he married Robert Arden's youngest daughter, Mary. Mary and John had four sons – William was the oldest – and four daughters, of whom only Joan outlived her most celebrated sibling. William was baptized (an event entered in the Stratford parish church records) on April 26, 1564, and it has become customary, without any good factual support, to suppose he was born on April 23, which happens to be the feast day of Saint George, patron saint of England, and is also the date on which he died, in 1616. Shakespeare married Anne Hathaway in 1582, when he was eighteen and she was twenty-six; their first child was born five months later. It has been generally assumed that the marriage was enforced and subsequently unhappy, but these are only assumptions; it has been estimated, for instance, that up to one third of Elizabethan brides were pregnant when they married. Anne and William Shakespeare had three children: Susanna, who married a prominent local physician, John Hall; and the twins Hamnet, who died young in 1596, and Judith, who married Thomas Quiney – apparently a rather shady individual. The name Hamnet was unusual but not unique: he and his twin sister were named for their godparents, Shakespeare's neighbors Hamnet and Judith Sadler. Shakespeare's father died in 1601 (the year of *Hamlet*), and Mary Arden Shakespeare died in 1608 (the year of *Coriolanus*). William Shakespeare's last surviving direct descendant was his granddaughter Elizabeth Hall, who died in 1670.

Between the birth of the twins in 1585 and a clear reference to Shakespeare as a practicing London dramatist in Robert Greene's sensationalizing, satiric pamphlet, *Greene's Groatsworth of Wit* (1592), there is no record of where William Shakespeare was or what he was doing. These seven so-called lost years have been imaginatively filled by scholars and other students of Shakespeare: some think he traveled to Italy, or fought in the Low Countries, or studied law or medicine, or worked as an apprentice actor/writer, and so on to even more fanciful possibilities. Whatever the biographical facts for those "lost" years, Greene's nasty remarks in 1592 testify to professional envy and to the fact that Shakespeare already had a successful career in London. Speaking to his fellow playwrights, Greene warns both generally and specifically:

> . . . trust them [actors] not: for there is an upstart crow, beautified with our feathers, that with his tiger's heart wrapped in a player's hide supposes he is as well able to bombast out a blank verse as the best of you; and being an absolute Johannes Factotum, is in his own conceit the only Shake-scene in a country.

The passage mimics a line from *3 Henry VI* (hence the play must have been performed before Greene wrote) and seems to say that "Shake-scene" is both actor and playwright, a jack-of-all-trades. That same year, Henry Chettle protested Greene's remarks in *Kind-Heart's Dream*, and each of the next two years saw the publication of poems – *Venus and Adonis* and *The Rape of Lucrece*, respectively – publicly ascribed to (and dedicated by) Shakespeare. Early in 1595 he was named one of the senior members of a prominent acting company, the Lord Chamberlain's Men, when they received payment for court performances during the 1594 Christmas season.

Clearly, Shakespeare had achieved both success and reputation in London. In 1596, upon Shakespeare's application, the College of Arms granted his father the now-familiar coat of arms he had taken the first steps to obtain almost twenty years before, and in 1598, John's son – now permitted to call himself "gentleman" – took a 10 percent share in the new Globe playhouse. In 1597, he bought a substantial bourgeois house, called New Place, in Stratford – the garden remains, but Shakespeare's house, several times rebuilt, was torn down in 1759 – and over the next few years Shakespeare spent large sums buying land and making other investments in the town and its environs. Though he worked in London, his family remained in Stratford, and he seems always to have considered Stratford the home he would eventually return to. Something approaching a disinterested appreciation of Shakespeare's popular and professional status appears in Francis Meres's *Palladis Tamia* (1598), a not especially imaginative and perhaps therefore persuasive record of literary reputations. Reviewing contemporary English writers, Meres lists the titles of many of Shakespeare's plays, including one not now known, *Love's Labor's Won,* and praises his "mellifluous & hony-tongued" "sugred Sonnets," which were then circulating in manuscript (they were first collected in 1609). Meres describes Shakespeare as "one of the best" English playwrights of both comedy and tragedy. In *Remains . . . Concerning Britain* (1605), William Camden – a more authoritative source than the imitative Meres – calls Shakespeare one of the "most pregnant witts of these our times" and joins him with such writers as Chapman, Daniel, Jonson, Marston, and Spenser. During the first decades of the seventeenth century, publishers began to attribute numerous play quartos, including some non-Shakespearean ones, to Shakespeare, either by name or initials, and we may assume that they deemed Shakespeare's name and supposed authorship, true or false, commercially attractive.

For the next ten years or so, various records show

Shakespeare's dual career as playwright and man of the theater in London, and as an important local figure in Stratford. In 1608-9 his acting company – designated the "King's Men" soon after King James had succeeded Queen Elizabeth in 1603 – rented, refurbished, and opened a small interior playing space, the Blackfriars theater, in London, and Shakespeare was once again listed as a substantial sharer in the group of proprietors of the playhouse. By May 11, 1612, however, he describes himself as a Stratford resident in a London lawsuit – an indication that he had withdrawn from day-to-day professional activity and returned to the town where he had always had his main financial interests. When Shakespeare bought a substantial residential building in London, the Blackfriars Gatehouse, close to the theater of the same name, on March 10, 1613, he is recorded as William Shakespeare "of Stratford upon Avon in the county of Warwick, gentleman," and he named several London residents as the building's trustees. Still, he continued to participate in theatrical activity: when the new Earl of Rutland needed an allegorical design to bear as a shield, or *impresa,* at the celebration of King James's Accession Day, March 24, 1613, the earl's accountant recorded a payment of 44 shillings to Shakespeare for the device with its motto.

For the last few years of his life, Shakespeare evidently concentrated his activities in the town of his birth. Most of the final records concern business transactions in Stratford, ending with the notation of his death on April 23, 1616, and burial in Holy Trinity Church, Stratford-upon-Avon.

THE QUESTION OF AUTHORSHIP

The history of ascribing Shakespeare's plays (the poems do not come up so often) to someone else began, as it continues, peculiarly. The earliest published claim that someone else wrote Shakespeare's plays appeared in an 1856 article by Delia Bacon in the American journal *Putnam's Monthly* – although an Englishman, Thomas Wilmot, had shared his doubts in private (even secretive) conversations with friends near the end of the eighteenth century. Bacon's was a sad personal history that ended in madness and poverty, but the year after her article, she published, with great difficulty and the bemused assistance of Nathaniel Hawthorne (then United States Consul in Liverpool, England), her *Philosophy of the Plays of Shakspere Unfolded.* This huge, ornately written, confusing farrago is almost unreadable; sometimes its intents, to say nothing of its arguments, disappear entirely beneath near-raving, ecstatic writing. Tumbled in with much supposed "philosophy" appear the claims that Francis Bacon (from whom Delia Bacon eventually claimed descent), Walter Ralegh, and several other contemporaries of Shakespeare's had written the plays. The book had little impact except as a ridiculed curiosity.

Once proposed, however, the issue gained momentum among people whose conviction was the greater in proportion to their ignorance of sixteenth- and seventeenth-century English literature, history, and society. Another American amateur, Catherine P. Ashmead Windle, made the next influential contribution to the cause when she published *Report to the British Museum* (1882), wherein she promised to open "the Cipher of Francis Bacon," though what she mostly offers, in the words of S. Schoenbaum, is "demented allegorizing." An entire new cottage industry grew from Windle's suggestion that the texts contain hidden, cryptographically discoverable ciphers – "clues" – to their authorship; and today there are not only books devoted to the putative ciphers, but also pamphlets, journals, and newsletters.

Although Baconians have led the pack of those seeking a substitute Shakespeare, in *"Shakespeare" Identified* (1920), J. Thomas Looney became the first published

"Oxfordian" when he proposed Edward de Vere, seventeenth earl of Oxford, as the secret author of Shakespeare's plays. Also for Oxford and his "authorship" there are today dedicated societies, articles, journals, and books. Less popular candidates – Queen Elizabeth and Christopher Marlowe among them – have had adherents, but the movement seems to have divided into two main contending factions, Baconian and Oxfordian. (For further details on all the candidates for "Shakespeare," see S. Schoenbaum, *Shakespeare's Lives,* 2nd ed., 1991.)

The Baconians, the Oxfordians, and supporters of other candidates have one trait in common – they are snobs. Every pro-Bacon or pro-Oxford tract sooner or later claims that the historical William Shakespeare of Stratford-upon-Avon could not have written the plays because he could not have had the training, the university education, the experience, and indeed the imagination or background their author supposedly possessed. Only a learned genius like Bacon or an aristocrat like Oxford could have written such fine plays. (As it happens, lucky male children of the middle class had access to better education than most aristocrats in Elizabethan England – and Oxford was not particularly well educated.) Shakespeare received in the Stratford grammar school a formal education that would daunt many college graduates today; and popular rival playwrights such as the very learned Ben Jonson and George Chapman, both of whom also lacked university training, achieved great artistic success, without being taken as Bacon or Oxford.

Besides snobbery, one other quality characterizes the authorship controversy: lack of evidence. A great deal of testimony from Shakespeare's time shows that Shakespeare wrote Shakespeare's plays and that his contemporaries recognized them as distinctive and distinctly superior. (Some of that contemporary evidence is collected in E. K. Chambers, *William Shakespeare: A Study of Facts and Problems,* 2 vols., 1930.) Since that testimony comes from Shakespeare's enemies and theatrical competitors as well as from his co-workers and from the Elizabethan equivalent of literary journalists, it seems unlikely that, if any one of these sources had known he was a fraud, they would have failed to record that fact.

Books About Shakespeare's Theater

Useful scholarly studies of theatrical life in Shakespeare's day include: G. E. Bentley, *The Jacobean and Caroline Stage*, 7 vols. (1941-68), and the same author's *The Professions of Dramatist and Player in Shakespeare's Time, 1590-1642* (1986); E. K. Chambers, *The Elizabethan Stage*, 4 vols. (1923); R. A. Foakes, *Illustrations of the English Stage, 1580-1642* (1985); Andrew Gurr, *The Shakespearean Stage*, 3rd ed. (1992), and the same author's *Play-going in Shakespeare's London*, 2nd ed. (1996); Edwin Nungezer, *A Dictionary of Actors* (1929); Carol Chillington Rutter, ed., *Documents of the Rose Playhouse* (1984).

Books About Shakespeare's Life

The following books provide scholarly, documented accounts of Shakespeare's life: G. E. Bentley, *Shakespeare: A Biographical Handbook* (1961); E. K. Chambers, *William Shakespeare: A Study of Facts and Problems*, 2 vols. (1930); S. Schoenbaum, *William Shakespeare: A Compact Documentary Life* (1977); and *Shakespeare's Lives*, 2nd ed. (1991), by the same author. Many scholarly editions of Shakespeare's complete works print brief compilations of essential dates and events. References to Shakespeare's works up to 1700 are collected in C. M. Ingleby et al., *The Shakespeare Allusion-Book*, rev. ed., 2 vols. (1932).

The Texts of Shakespeare

As far as we know, only one manuscript conceivably in Shakespeare's own hand may (and even this is much disputed) exist: a few pages of a play called *Sir Thomas More,* which apparently was never performed. What we do have, as later readers, performers, scholars, students, are printed texts. The earliest of these survive in two forms: quartos and folios. Quartos (from the Latin for "four") are small books, printed on sheets of paper that were then folded twice, to make four leaves or eight pages. When these were bound together, the result was a squarish, eminently portable volume that sold for the relatively small sum of sixpence (translating in modern terms to about $5.00). In folios, on the other hand, the sheets are folded only once, in half, producing large, impressive volumes taller than they are wide. This was the format for important works of philosophy, science, theology, and literature (the major precedent for a folio Shakespeare was Ben Jonson's *Works,* 1616). The decision to print the works of a popular playwright in folio is an indication of how far up on the social scale the theatrical profession had come during Shakespeare's lifetime. The Shakespeare folio was an expensive book, selling for between fifteen and eighteen shillings, depending on the binding (in modern terms, from about $150 to $180). Twenty Shakespeare plays of the thirty-seven that survive first appeared in quarto, seventeen of which appeared during Shakespeare's lifetime; the rest of the plays are found only in folio.

The First Folio was published in 1623, seven years after Shakespeare's death, and was authorized by his fellow actors, the co-owners of the King's Men. This publication was certainly a mark of the company's enormous respect for Shakespeare; but it was also a way of turning the old plays, most of which were no longer current in the play-house, into ready money (the folio includes only Shakespeare's plays, not his sonnets or other nondramatic verse). Whatever the motives behind the publication of the folio, the texts it preserves constitute the basis for almost all later editions of the playwright's works. The texts, however, differ from those of the earlier quartos, sometimes in minor respects but often significantly – most strikingly in the two texts of *King Lear,* but also in important ways in *Hamlet, Othello,* and *Troilus and Cressida.* (The variants are recorded in the textual notes to each play in the new Pelican series.) The differences in these texts represent, in a sense, the essence of theater: the texts of plays were initially not intended for publication. They were scripts, designed for the actors to perform – the principal life of the play at this period was in performance. And it follows that in Shakespeare's theater the playwright typically had no say either in how his play was performed or in the disposition of his text – he was an employee of the company. The authoritative figures in the theatrical enterprise were the shareholders in the company, who were for the most part the major actors. They decided what plays were to be done; they hired the playwright and often gave him an outline of the play they wanted him to write. Often, too, the play was a collaboration: the company would retain a group of writers, and parcel out the scenes among them. The resulting script was then the property of the company, and the actors would revise it as they saw fit during the course of putting it on stage. The resulting text belonged to the company. The playwright had no rights in it once he had been paid. (This system survives largely intact in the movie industry, and most of the playwrights of Shakespeare's time were as anonymous as most screenwriters are today.) The script could also, of course, continue to change as the tastes of audiences and the requirements of the actors changed. Many – perhaps most – plays were revised when they were reintroduced after any substantial absence from the repertory, or when they were performed by a company different from the one that originally commissioned the play.

Shakespeare was an exceptional figure in this world because he was not only a shareholder and actor in his company, but also its leading playwright – he was literally his own boss. He had, moreover, little interest in the publication of his plays, and even those that appeared during his lifetime with the authorization of the company show no signs of any editorial concern on the part of the author. Theater was, for Shakespeare, a fluid and supremely responsive medium – the very opposite of the great classic canonical text that has embodied his works since 1623.

The very fluidity of the original texts, however, has meant that Shakespeare has always had to be edited. Here is an example of how problematic the editorial project inevitably is, a passage from the most famous speech in *Romeo and Juliet,* Juliet's balcony soliloquy beginning "O Romeo, Romeo, wherefore art thou Romeo?" Since the eighteenth century, the standard modern text has read,

> What's Montague? It is nor hand, nor foot,
> Nor arm, nor face, nor any other part
> Belonging to a man. O be some other name!
> What's in a name? That which we call a rose
> By any other name would smell as sweet.
>
> (II.2.40–44)

Editors have three early texts of this play to work from, two quarto texts and the folio. Here is how the First Quarto (1597) reads:

> Whats *Mountague?* It is nor band nor foote,
> Nor arme, nor face, nor any other part.
> Whats in a name? That which we call a Rofe,
> By any other name would fmell as fweet:

Here is the Second Quarto (1599):

> Whats *Mountague*? it is nor hand nor foote,
> Nor arme nor face, ô be some other name
> Belonging to a man.
> Whats in a name that which we call a rose,
> By any other word would smell as sweete,

And here is the First Folio (1623):

> What's *Mountague*? it is nor hand nor foote,
> Nor arme, nor face, O be some other name
> Belonging to a man.
> What? in a names that which we call a Rose,
> By any other word would smell as sweete,

There is in fact no early text that reads as our modern text does – and this is the most famous speech in the play. Instead, we have three quite different texts, all of which are clearly some version of the same speech, but none of which seems to us a final or satisfactory version. The transcendently beautiful passage in modern editions is an editorial invention: editors have succeeded in conflating and revising the three versions into something we recognize as great poetry. Is this what Shakespeare "really" wrote? Who can say? What we can say is that Shakespeare always had performance, not a book, in mind.

Books About the Shakespeare Texts

The standard study of the printing history of the First Folio is W. W. Greg, *The Shakespeare First Folio* (1955). J. K. Walton, *The Quarto Copy for the First Folio of Shakespeare* (1971), is a useful survey of the relation of the quartos to the folio. The second edition of Charlton Hinman's *Norton Facsimile* of the First Folio (1996), with a new introduction by Peter Blayney, is indispensable. Stanley Wells and Gary Taylor, *William Shakespeare: A Textual Companion,* keyed to the Oxford text, gives a comprehensive survey of the editorial situation for all the plays and poems.

THE GENERAL EDITORS

Introduction

IN 1616, Shakespeare's contemporary Ben Jonson published a large volume containing his own collected works, the first time an English playwright had made such an emphatic statement about the worth of his writing. At the head of the volume he placed the earliest of his plays that he was prepared to acknowledge, *Every Man in His Humour.* Seven years later, in 1623, John Heminges and Henry Condell, two of Shakespeare's friends and fellow actors, collected together Shakespeare's plays and published *Mr. William Shakespeares Comedies, Histories & Tragedies,* the book now known as the First Folio. The first play in the volume is *The Tempest,* probably the last play wholly written by Shakespeare.

When Jonson's play was first performed in 1598, it was set in Italy. But in his *Works* he printed a revised version, with the action transposed to London. Shakespeare's play is set, according to his editors, on "an uninhabited island." The revised *Every Man in His Humour* reflects the teeming density of life in a great city, finding there the versions of human behavior that Jonson wished to display in the theater. If Jonson's characters are often derived from comic stereotypes and classical comedy, they live in a London that is bursting with the details of the streets just outside the theaters where the play was performed. *The Tempest* seeks to examine human behavior in a world that proves, with increasingly dizzying paradoxicality, to be both real and unreal, actual and artifice. For the world through which the characters move is both a creation of Prospero's magic art and something beyond that art, in exactly the same way that their desires and intentions prove variously to be within the scope of Prospero's manipulation or frustratingly beyond it.

Jonson was never reconciled to the art of Shakespeare's last plays. In *Bartholomew Fair* (1614), performed four years after *The Tempest* was written, one of the characters is named Mooncalf, a word twice used in *The Tempest* by Stephano to describe Caliban in II.2, a mocking transposition of Shakespeare's strangest character to a London fair. As a character speaking for Jonson announces in the Induction to *Bartholomew Fair,* with a sideswipe at Shakespeare, "He is loath to make Nature afraid in his plays, like those that beget Tales, Tempests, and such like drolleries," and we can catch here an echo of Sebastian's description of the appearance of the "several strange Shapes" who bring in a banquet in III.3: "A living drollery." For Jonson there was nothing more weird and wonderful to be found on "an uninhabited island" than could be found in the middle of London. But for Shakespeare, the island is the laboratory in which human activity, including that of the scientist himself, can best be put under the microscope.

Of course the First Folio is wrong: the island is not uninhabited. Tracing its inhabitants reflects on where the island is. Before Prospero and Miranda had arrived there, the island had been colonized by Sycorax, then pregnant with Caliban, and her "airy spirit" servant Ariel, after she had been exiled from Algiers. Prospero, thrown out of his dukedom, Milan, by his usurping brother, finds his rotten boat lands him on the island, now solely inhabited by and ruled over by Caliban, who was "mine own king" – though can one rule if one has no subjects? Alonso and the other lords who have accompanied him to Tunis for his daughter's wedding are sailing home from Tunis to Naples when they come within the orbit of Prospero's magic and are brought to the island. All these sea voyages are across the Mediterranean.

Magic islands do not necessarily have a fixed place on a map. But the fact that Ariel is sent by Prospero "to fetch dew / From the still-vexed Bermudas" (I.2.228-29), taken together with some of the sources Shakespeare used and the play's evident interest in the problem of colonization, has led many to assume that the play is set somewhere close to America. But the geography may suggest the reverse: not that Europeans are now confronting the New World in the interests of exploration and empire but that elements of that New World, which imperialist discoverers had encountered – the natural abundance and the indigenous population – are now transposed to the Old World, a world that is sustainedly aware of its roots in Roman civilization and its narratives of empire.

For *The Tempest* makes careful use of its deliberately placed echoes of classical narratives. A play in which Claribel has been married in the city where Dido ruled and died when abandoned by Aeneas, and in which Ferdinand's first words about Miranda, "Most sure, the goddess" (I.2.422), translate words of Aeneas in Virgil's *Aeneid,* is clearly evoking an epic narrative of the voyaging and the founding of empire. A play in which Prospero describes his frightening magical powers (V.1.33-50) in a remarkably close use of Medea's invocation in Ovid's *Metamorphoses* (Book 7) and Arthur Golding's 1567 translation is clearly transmuting her evil response to being a rejected lover in a strange land. A play in which Gonzalo promises to rule his ideal commonwealth so well as "T' excel the golden age" (II.1.168) is reminding its audience of the perfect world, the prelapsarian ideal detailed by Ovid in the first book of *Metamorphoses.*

Gonzalo's vision of a utopic state comes almost word for word from John Florio's 1603 translation of Michel de Montaigne's essay "Of the Cannibals" (Book 1, Chapter 30, of his *Essays*). Montaigne saw the perfect existence of the native peoples – as he heard about it – as the embodiment of a Golden Age not in some mythic past but in a present distant only in its geography. But Montaigne is also seeing a conjunction between Ovid's myth and the reality of a world of which Ovid knew nothing. The classical myth and the reports of Elizabethan voyagers converge. *The Tempest* encourages us to compare and contrast

Gonzalo's golden age with that beneficent world displayed in the betrothal masque Prospero stages for Ferdinand and Miranda, an image of a world where nymphs and reapers meet and dance, presided over by Roman deities who offer a future of "Honor, riches, marriage blessing, / Long continuance, and increasing" (IV.1.106-7), in which the natural world controlled by Ceres with "Barns and garners never empty" will be made available for the lovers as much as the island offers its own resources for everyone on it.

The Tempest is one of a remarkably small number of Shakespeare plays for which no narrative or dramatic source for the action has been identified. But Shakespeare did make extensive use of Elizabethan travel writing both for the depiction of the confrontation of the Europeans and a "savage" and for his dramatization of the opening storm. In particular he used William Strachey's account, written in 1610 though not published until 1625, of the shipwreck and "redemption" of Sir Thomas Gates in the Bermudas. Gates was wrecked in a "most dreadful tempest" on an island that was so pleasant and so full of food that some of his crew conspired to stop Gates's attempts to leave the island and head toward Jamestown. Shakespeare owes some of the realist detail of the storm in I.1 to Strachey's letter, but he also found in it an island that, far from being "no habitation for men but rather given over to devils and wicked spirits," proved to Strachey "to be as habitable and commodious as most countries of the same climate and situation."

Prospero's island is a metamorphic world of contrasts. Adrian finds that its air "breathes upon us here most sweetly" while Sebastian thinks it smells "As if it had lungs, and rotten ones"; Gonzalo finds its grass "lush and lusty" while Antonio sees it as "tawny" (II.1.47-55). Caliban offers to show Trinculo and Stephano "the best springs" and where to find interesting food (II.2.157-69), just as, years earlier, he had shown Prospero "all the qualities o' th' isle" (I.2.337). But the three conspirators follow the unseen Ariel through "Toothed briers, sharp furzes, pricking gorse, and thorns" until they are left up to their chins in a "filthy mantled pool" (IV.1.180-82). By turns benign and generous in its provision of natural goodness and viciously unyielding in its treatment of its new immigrants, the island seems to reflect, as so much in the play does, the different perceptions of its visitors and the changeable moods of Prospero. Prospero is able to impose onto the island a kind of double perspective so that the naturally abundant becomes, through his art, troublingly intransigent.

The ambivalence is strongest in the treatment – both by Prospero and by Shakespeare – of Ariel and Caliban. The cast list of *The Tempest* is small, but it is full of intriguing and uneasy reflections. Sycorax, for instance, is a distorted mirroring of Prospero, proficient like him in the magic arts and exiled like him with a child. Whereas Sycorax was banished for "mischiefs manifold and sorceries terrible" (I.2.264), Prospero was banished because he had abandoned rule to his brother to devote himself to study, his neglect of the proper discharge of his authority creating the space that enabled Antonio to plot his overthrow. On the island both Sycorax and Prospero have enslaved and ill-treated Ariel, Sycorax imprisoning him in a cloven pine, while Prospero compels him into an apprenticeship that comes to an end at the end of the play. If Prospero's treatment seems less brutal, more in line with the experience of any indentured servant in London, it still means that Ariel is "my slave" (I.2.270). Ariel may be a spirit, but he is both a recognizable analogy to and a representative of the contemporary English servant class.

He is also, though not human, able both to recognize the appropriate human emotions of compassion and pity for the lords maddened on Prospero's orders and to encourage those emotions in the previously unyielding Prospero. "Bountiful Fortune / (Now, my dear lady)" has enabled Prospero to have his enemies at his mercy. But once he has separated them from the others, he seems not to have a clear plan what he wants to do with them. In a drama whose organization of the characters into groups is entirely dependent on Prospero's control and whose form is strongly patterned into abstract shapes, it is surprising that the action is not apparently similarly shaped. The play's form continually suggests a spatial structure of mirrors rather than a linear shape. But the final move to a pitying response to others' pain, to a humane recognition of a higher virtue than vengeance, has to come from outside Prospero, from a character who cannot share the feelings Ariel enables Prospero to find in himself.

Sycorax imprisoned Ariel for his refusal to obey her orders. Prospero enslaved Caliban for what he saw as the attempted rape of his daughter. Miranda has been educated on the island in the manners and ethics of her courtly background, the beliefs of a culture that sees itself as civilized. Caliban, born on the island, is a figure who acts from a set of appetites and desires that the play sees as natural, as pre-social. The cast list's labeling him as a "savage and deformed slave" epitomizes the clash of perspectives. First treated caringly while a child, educated into language and offering love in return, Caliban has now been enslaved for an act of uncivilized desire. His attempt to "violate / The honor" of Miranda (I.2.347-48) may have seemed, from his point of view, less like an attempted rape than the response of a natural sexuality that cannot comprehend the concern with sexual honor so dear to Prospero and his culture.

Gonzalo's perfect commonwealth assumed free but innocent sexual activity (or, as Antonio inevitably sees it, "all idle – whores and knaves"), but Caliban's desire is not allowed to be innocent. Though Miranda's distaste for the idea of sex with Caliban is entirely understandable, Caliban is left with an unrealized desire to have "peopled . . . / This isle with Calibans," not, of course, with Mirandas. Whereas Romantic critics tended to allegorize Caliban as brute appetite contrasted with the airy imagination of Ariel, we may perhaps be readier to see him as a character caught in a colonialist trap, dehumanized and forced into service yet retaining a certain unregenerate rebelliousness. When given the chance to escape from Prospero's control, he can, however, imagine nothing more radical than replacing one master with another, Stephano.

The stage history of Caliban reflects the ambivalences that surround the character. Often, particularly at the end of the last century, played as subhuman, more ape than man (Frank Benson's costume in the 1890s was described by his wife as "half monkey, half coconut"), he has also become reptilian, so that James Earl Jones's Caliban in 1962 could be described as "a savage, green-faced lizard." More recently he has often been played by black actors, emphasizing the colonialist view of the play, the actor's skin symbolizing the character's oppression. But Tony Haygarth's Caliban in 1988 at the Royal National Theatre in London combined the contrasts: hints of devil's horns sprouted on his head while his back was bleeding from Prospero's treatment of him, and his genitals were encased in a brutal box, a visible punishment for the attack on Miranda but one that said more of the punisher's fear of sexuality than the crime of the punished.

Such doubleness is a reflection of Caliban's language in the play. Prospero and Miranda have taught him language and, if one "profit on't / Is I know how to curse" (I.2.363–64), it also enables him to speak with transfixing delight of both the pleasures of the island and the painful frustrations of its magical world of noises that lull Caliban back into sleep, giving him his own wonderful dreams in which

> The clouds methought would open and show riches
> Ready to drop upon me, that, when I waked,
> I cried to dream again.
>
> (III.2.140–42)

These "sounds and sweet airs" are harmless: they "give delight and hurt not." But Caliban's more common experience of the island is as a place of brutality where he will be pinched and cramped, brutalized by unseen spirits, and tormented till he roars in pain. *The Tempest* may be a play full of music, but its musicians are usually unseen, its effect is unnerving, and its sound score is equally full of the cries of those hurt by Prospero's punishments.

Caliban shares with Ariel a perception of the distinction between the natural reality of the island and those phenomena that are the product of Prospero's art. The spirits that may pinch Caliban cannot harm him "unless he bid 'em" (II.2.7). In his clear understanding Caliban knows more than the audience. The play opens with a tempest that is depicted with all the realistic effects at the disposal of the theater. The sound effects, the appearance of the sailors "wet," the cries of instruction from the Boatswain all create an illusion of a ship at sea more brilliantly than in any other contemporary play. Only at the beginning of the next scene can the audience realize that the "tempestuous noise of thunder and lightning" is created by Prospero's art. Productions that show Prospero creating the storm or show Ariel as he "flamed amazement" (I.2.198) miss the point. The audience needs to be disoriented, to be made unsure what can be defined as natural and what an example of Prospero's magic arts. In the disturbing conjunction of the artful and the artless, Shakespeare stretches the limits of the real.

Realizing it was fooled by the theatrically realistic power of the first scene, the audience may be more reluctant to be confident in a judgment of subsequent events and an assessment of individuals' subsequent action. But often *The Tempest* refuses to make clear whether an event has Prospero's art behind it. When the King of Naples and most of his party fall asleep in II.1, is the audience to understand that Prospero is responsible for the fact that Antonio and Sebastian do not sleep? Does he intend to give them the opportunity to hatch a conspiracy that recapitulates in little the expulsion of Prospero from Milan (though this time with the darker threat of murder rather

than exile)? The later transformation of these two conspirators into the murderous triumvirate of Caliban, Trinculo, and Stephano is another of the play's mirrors. If
Trinculo and Stephano are clowns, figures of comic fun,
they are enmeshed in a "foul conspiracy" of murder no
different from the plans of Antonio and Sebastian and
graphically described by Caliban: "there thou mayst brain
him, /. . . or with a log / Batter his skull, or paunch him
with a stake, / Or cut his wesand with thy knife"
(III.2.87–90).

All the conspirators share the same ambition of rule, be
it over Naples and Milan or over the island. The lust for
power is widely shared, even by Prospero. If the experience of being subject to Prospero's control is for some,
like Alonso, transforming and beneficial, an opportunity
to explore themselves in some fantastical version of psy-
chotherapy, then for others Prospero's resolution of the
action changes nothing. Silence fascinates Shakespeare,
even in his theater of language and noise. There is nothing in Antonio's few brief comments in the last scene to
suggest that he is in the least the "penitent" Prospero as-
sumes or hopes all the King's party have become. In
W. H. Auden's long poem *The Sea and the Mirror,* in
many ways the most brilliantly creative response *The
Tempest* has generated, Antonio is allowed to voice what
Shakespeare leaves ambiguously silent, his rejection of
Prospero's forgiveness:

> Your all is partial, Prospero;
>   My will is all my own:
> Your need to love shall never know
> Me: I am I, Antonio,
>   By choice myself alone.

Auden's view of Antonio's recalcitrance, his intransigent
refusal to give in to the demands of Prospero's will – for
even the offer of forgiveness is an expression of Prospero's
power – suggests an Antonio who is even more deserving

than Caliban of Prospero's description of the latter as one "on whose nature / Nurture can never stick" (IV.1.188-89). It is not only the uncivilized man who can reject the values aspired to by civilized society. *The Tempest* has spawned a number of attempts by other dramatists to continue the narrative: they clearly distrusted the resolution of the action, and all anticipated a further rebellion against a Prospero now devoid of his magic arts.

As ruler of the island and as magus, learned in the arts of power, Prospero attains as much control as Renaissance culture could imagine any human being achieving. Gonzalo's charitable act, putting into the exiles' boat "Rich garments, linens, stuffs, and necessaries / Which since have steaded much" (I.2.164-65), helped the castaways to survive, and provided the clothes that so attract Trinculo and Stephano that they are diverted from their plan of murder. But Gonzalo also, "Knowing I loved my books . . . furnished me / From mine own library with volumes that / I prize above my dukedom" (I.2.166-68). *The Tempest* celebrates the awesome power contained in books, the whole world of secret, cabalistic knowledge that might lead to the power over unknown forces that Prospero is able to unleash. When the filmmaker Peter Greenaway wanted to explore the play and the new technologies of video, he concentrated on Prospero's library; his brilliant film *Prospero's Books* (1991) is a melancholic celebration of books that contain knowledge of a kind we have lost.

Prospero's power has been learned from his books, which at the end of the play he will drown, and is exerted through the magic robe he wears and the staff that he carries onstage and will finally break. But for the duration of the play his power has reached an extent that is almost blasphemous. Prospero has been able not only to raise storms and release a spirit imprisoned in a cloven pine but also to raise the dead: "graves at my command / Have waked their sleepers, oped, and let 'em forth / By my so potent art" (V.1.48-50). His art has given him power that extends far beyond fake meteorological tricks. He has carefully informed Miranda – and the audience – that his storm has done no harm at all to the mariners, "not so much perdition as an hair" (I.2.30), though in modern circumstances they would no doubt litigate for the psychological trauma. But waking the dead usurps actions that Christ will perform at the Last Judgment. Prospero's rough magic is dangerous knowledge; the return to the normative limits of human power will be difficult: "Now my charms are all o'erthrown, / And what strength I have's mine own, / Which is most faint" (Epilogue, 1-3). Yet even at this moment, there is a disconcerting echo of Christ. Prospero is not a savior but he ends the play, as Christ ended life, in the full awareness of his weak humanity.

Apparently limitless in his control of the physical and metaphysical universe (at least within the force field of the island), Prospero is able to summon up powers that other mortals cannot even see. Only when he appears as Ceres or as a harpy – another echo of Virgil – can Ariel be seen by mortals other than Prospero. His disguise as a sea nymph is only for Prospero's and the audience's delight, for he will be "invisible / To every eyeball else" (I.2.302-3). But Prospero cannot control the effects of his powers on human feelings. This is not only a negative limitation in the impossibility of changing Antonio against his will. It is also the wonderful positive of Ferdinand and Miranda's love, an outpouring of innocent and joyous emotion that Prospero hoped for but could not create. At the play's center, in III.1, comes a depiction of joyful service. Surrounding this central panel, the other scenes link before and after in pairs defined by the groups of characters in them: Caliban, Stephano, and Trinculo in II.2 and III.2; Alonso, Sebastian, and Antonio in II.1 and III.3; Prospero, Ferdinand, and Miranda ending I.2 and beginning IV.1. Opening with Ferdinand bearing logs – as the previous scene had begun with Caliban doing the same work – this central scene contrasts willing work to win the right to marry the woman Ferdinand loves with unwilling work forced on Caliban because he had attempted to have sex with the same woman. The scene's "encounter / Of two most rare affections" (74-75) is the pinnacle of Prospero's pleasure: "my rejoicing / At nothing can be more" (93-94).

As a reward for this love, Prospero offers them a betrothal masque, "Some vanity of mine art" (IV.1.41). Prospero's art dominates the play, for it is unashamedly theatrical. It can vary from the spectacle of the storm to the spectacle of the masque, from the extreme realism of the one to the formalism of magnificent court entertainment. Masques were seventeenth-century theatricality at their most opulent limit of performance. Their displays of wealth and commentaries on power were exhibited through the arts of sight and sound, sets and music. Performed on a single occasion, masques might seem the quintessence of ephemerality, but Prospero argues that there is no difference between their transience and that of everything else in existence, which "shall dissolve, / And, like this insubstantial pageant faded, / Leave not a rack behind" (IV.1.154-56).

With Prospero as stage manager and master of the revels, the island is a confined space that his melancholic vision sees as resonating with universal evanescence. The brief show with which he celebrates and attempts to bless the love of Ferdinand and Miranda cannot achieve the normal fulfillment of a masque, the moment of the revels when the actors and the spectators join together in dance to proclaim, through their actions, an image of harmony. Prospero's forgetfulness of the Caliban conspiracy, the sense that for the first time in the play there is something evil over which he no longer can maintain control, disrupts the masque and the patterning of scenes that has dominated the play's formal organization. But a celebration of the ending of the play cannot occur so early, for it is only Act IV.

In the public theaters of London like the Globe, a performance was continuous. The absence of act intervals makes the perception of five-act structure difficult. Often Shakespeare seems not to have been concerned to structure his plays in anything approaching a five-act rhythm. There had been exceptions: the Chorus in *Henry V* opens each act, but the difficulty he has in controlling the play's geographical movements and the disjunctions between what he describes and what the next scene shows argue that the form is in fundamental tension with the messiness of history. By the time *The Tempest* was performed, the King's Men, Shakespeare's company, were also using the Blackfriars theater, and had adopted the practice of music between the acts, standard in such roofed, private theaters.

The Tempest is a play peculiarly conscious of its own time scale and form, a form largely created by Prospero as well as Shakespeare. It is Prospero who decides that the play shall obey unity of time, defining Ariel's limit of slavery as coterminous with the length of the play's performance. The reminders of time passing would be odd in any other Shakespeare play: there may be "no clock in the forest" of Arden in *As You Like It,* but Prospero will spend the "time 'twixt six and now" on his plots (I.2.240), and even the sleepy Boatswain knows in Act V that it is "but three glasses since" he announced the boat had split (V.1.223) – three hours, that is, since the play's first scene. It is Prospero, as much as Shakespeare, who keeps the three groups of shipwrecked travelers apart until the appearance of Caliban and company after the masque disrupts the play's patterning and until all the human characters are able to encounter one another in the final scene, where even the Master and Boatswain are able to reappear. There is almost a vanity of Prospero's art in trying to make everything take place in such an inordinately short expanse of fictional time, a virtuosic demonstration of his manipulative skills.

But, like love and conspiracy, the ending is not quite in Prospero's control. Indeed, when it finally comes, the play's ending is notably incomplete. Alonso does not know that Prospero has been responsible for the experiences that Alonso's party has undergone, that Prospero is the "oracle" who "Must rectify our knowledge" (V.1.244-45). The journey home must, of course, lie beyond the bounds of the play, as it lies beyond the bounds of the island, but Prospero makes Alonso a promise that he cannot be sure of fulfilling: "calm seas, auspicious gales, / And sail so expeditious that shall catch / Your royal fleet far off" (315-17). For in the Epilogue Prospero has to ask for the audience's help: its applause and cheers will free him from the island and provide the wind that "my sails / Must fill, or else my project fails" (11-12).

Shakespeare had rarely written epilogues before, but he had never written one in which the speaker is a character still trapped in the plot. At the end of *As You Like It* the actor playing Rosalind steps out from behind the character, offering to kiss us "If I were a woman" and thereby reminding us of the gender of the performer, not the gender of the character. At the end of *All's Well That Ends Well,* the actor playing the King of France tells us, "The king's a beggar now the play is done." Such reminders of the limits of the fictional world of performance are impossible in *The Tempest,* where Shakespeare has emphasized an identity between the stage and the world. Prospero, not the actor, must try to conjure again without his magical powers, asking us for a storm of applause to balance the storm of the first scene. He asks us for his liberty, as he had been asked by Ariel to release him at the beginning of the play. Throughout the play characters have been enslaved by Prospero: Caliban and Ariel, Ferdinand and his father, Antonio and Sebastian. Now the play's slave master asks for mercy by calling on the audience's own need: "As you from crimes would pardoned be, / Let your indulgence set me free."

Prospero has been removed from the other human characters in all three of the roles he has played. As monarch colonizing and ruling the island, as magus-scientist controlling his experiment with superhuman forces, as theatrical creator making the humans perform as characters in his play, he has sustained a removedness. But Prospero must finally come to some kind of awareness of what has occurred and how it affects him. Lying behind his tormented account to Miranda in I.2 of the events leading to his exile, the unacted beginning of the play's narrative, are years of repression of that knowledge. When Prospero tells Miranda, it is as if he tells himself for the first time, as if he voices what has been unspoken for twelve years. The contradictoriness of the account, the ambiguities between the blame for his own negligence and the indictment of Antonio, should worry us if we pay careful attention. Prospero's multiple roles support his authority: as playwright, as magus, and as king. In abandoning his art and his island rule he will turn again into a duke, not a king, and appear "As I was sometime Milan" (V.1.86). Shorn of the otherness of his power and its symbols of robe and staff, Prospero in the last scene can often appear in productions oddly disappointing, a little too ordinary when wearing the hat and rapier he orders Ariel to fetch. After the vastnesses of the play's compass, after the distances the mind imaginatively travels outside the island, Prospero's appearance may bring us down to earth with something of a bump. Going out of the theater, the first audience found itself in Jonson's London, a city that may have been reassuringly mundane. *The Tempest* peoples its uninhabited island with a range of characters and concepts that Jonson never comprehended.

PETER HOLLAND
The Shakespeare Institute,
The University of Birmingham

Note on the Text

*T*HE *TEMPEST* was first printed in the folio of 1623, evidently from a transcript (made by the scrivener Ralph Crane) of Shakespeare's draft after it had been prepared for production. The play stands first in the volume, in a carefully edited and printed text, supplied with unusually full stage directions, and a list of characters (following the Epilogue). The present edition follows the folio text; except for occasional relineation, departures from it are few and slight. The act-scene division supplied marginally is that of the folio. Below are listed all substantive departures from the folio text, with the adopted reading in italics followed by the folio reading in roman.

The Scene . . . Island followed by *Names of the Actors* (appears after Epilogue in F)

I.1 34 *Exeunt* Exit 36 *plague* plague – 49–50 *courses! Off* courses off 59–61 *Mercy . . . split* (assigned to Gonzalo in F) 62 *with th' king* with 'King

I.2 100 *unto* into 112 *with th' King* with King 159 *divine.* divine 201 *lightnings* Lightning 248 *made no* made thee no 271 *wast* was 282 *she* he 374 s.d. *ARIEL [Sings.]* Ariel Song 380 *the burden bear* beare the burthen 381 *Hark, hark!* (appears after s.d. *Burthen dispersedly* in l. 379 in F) 383 s.d. *Burden, dispersedly* (not in F) 396 s.d. *ARIEL [Sings.]* Ariell Song

II.1 s.d. *Francisco* Francisco, and others 5 *master* Masters 36 *Ha, ha, ha!* (assigned to Sebastian in F) 37 *So, you're paid* (assigned to Antonio in F) 64 *gloss* glosses 94 *Ay* I

II.2 45 (F has s.d. *Sings*) 177 *CALIBAN* (omitted in F)

III.1 2 *sets* set 15 *busilest* busie lest 93 *withal* with all

III.2 15 *on, by this light. Thou* on, by this light thou 51–52 *isle; From me* Isle From me, 121 *scout* cout

III.3 s.d. *Francisco* Francisco, &c 17 *SEBASTIAN . . . more* (appears after s.d. *Solemne . . . depart* in F) 19 s.d. *Enter . . . depart* (after 17 s.d. in F) 29 *islanders* Islands 65 *plume* plumbe

IV.1 9 *off* of   13 *gift* guest   17 *rite* right   52 *rein* raigne   74 s.d. (F has
s.d. *Iuno descends* by l.72)   74 *her* here   106 *marriage blessing* marriage,
blessing   145 *anger so* anger, so   193 s.d. *Enter Ariel . . . etc.* (appears
after *line* in F); *them on* on them   231 *Let't* let's
V.1 60 *boiled* boile   72 *Didst* Did   75 *entertained* entertaine   76 *who*
whom   82 *lies* ly   124 *not* nor   136 *who* whom   199 *remembrance* re-
membrances   248 *Which shall be shortly, single I'll* (Which shall be
shortly single) I'le   258 *coragio* Corasio

The Tempest

NAMES OF THE ACTORS

ALONSO, *King of Naples*
SEBASTIAN, *his brother*
PROSPERO, *the right Duke of Milan*
ANTONIO, *his brother, the usurping Duke of Milan*
FERDINAND, *son to the King of Naples*
GONZALO, *an honest old councilor*
ADRIAN AND FRANCISCO, *lords*
CALIBAN, *a savage and deformed slave*
TRINCULO, *a jester*
STEPHANO, *a drunken butler*
MASTER OF A SHIP
BOATSWAIN
MARINERS
MIRANDA, *daughter to Prospero*
ARIEL, *an airy spirit*
IRIS
CERES
JUNO   } *[personated by] spirits*
NYMPHS
REAPERS
[OTHER SPIRITS ATTENDING ON PROSPERO]

THE SCENE: *An uninhabited Island*
*

personated presented

The Tempest

❧ I.1 *A tempestuous noise of thunder and lightning heard. Enter a Shipmaster and a Boatswain.*

MASTER Boatswain!

BOATSWAIN Here, master. What cheer?

MASTER Good, speak to th' mariners; fall to't yarely, or 3
we run ourselves aground. Bestir, bestir!   *Exit.*
Enter Mariners.

BOATSWAIN Heigh, my hearts! Cheerly, cheerly, my
hearts! Yare, yare! Take in the topsail! Tend to th' mas- 6
ter's whistle! Blow till thou burst thy wind, if room 7
enough!
Enter Alonso, Sebastian, Antonio, Ferdinand,
Gonzalo, and others.

ALONSO Good boatswain, have care. Where's the mas-
ter? Play the men.   10

BOATSWAIN I pray now, keep below.

ANTONIO Where is the master, bos'n?

BOATSWAIN Do you not hear him? You mar our labor.
Keep your cabins: you do assist the storm.

GONZALO Nay, good, be patient.

BOATSWAIN When the sea is. Hence! What cares these
roarers for the name of king? To cabin! Silence! Trouble 17
us not!

I.1 The deck of a ship at sea 3 *Good* good fellow; *yarely* quickly 6 *Tend*
attend 7 *Blow . . . wind* (addressed to the storm) 7–8 *if room enough* i.e.,
so long as we have sea room 10 *Play the men* act like men 17 *roarers* (1)
waves, (2) rioters

GONZALO Good, yet remember whom thou hast
20 aboard.

BOATSWAIN None that I more love than myself. You are
a councilor: if you can command these elements to silence and work the peace of the present, we will not
24 hand a rope more; use your authority. If you cannot,
give thanks you have lived so long, and make yourself
ready in your cabin for the mischance of the hour, if it
so hap. – Cheerly, good hearts! – Out of our way, I say.

Exit.

GONZALO I have great comfort from this fellow: me-
29 thinks he hath no drowning mark upon him; his com-
30 plexion is perfect gallows. Stand fast, good Fate, to his
31 hanging! Make the rope of his destiny our cable, for
32 our own doth little advantage. If he be not born to be
hanged, our case is miserable.   *Exeunt.*

Enter Boatswain.

BOATSWAIN Down with the topmast! Yare! Lower, lower!
35 Bring her to try with main course! *(A cry within.)* A
36 plague upon this howling! They are louder than the
37 weather or our office.

Enter Sebastian, Antonio, and Gonzalo.

Yet again? What do you here? Shall we give o'er and
drown? Have you a mind to sink?

40 SEBASTIAN A pox o' your throat, you bawling, blasphemous, incharitable dog!

BOATSWAIN Work you, then.

ANTONIO Hang, cur, hang, you whoreson, insolent
noisemaker! We are less afraid to be drowned than thou
art.

---

24 *hand* handle 29–30 *complexion* indication of character in appearance of
face 30 *gallows* (alluding to the proverb "He that's born to be hanged need
fear no drowning") 31 *cable* anchor cable 32 *doth little advantage* doesn't
help us much 35 *try with main course* lie hove-to (close to the wind) with
only the mainsail 36 *plague* (followed by a dash in F, possibly indicating a
string of oaths censored out of the text; cf. l. 40, and V.1.218–19) 37 *our
office* (the noise we make at) our work

GONZALO   I'll warrant him for drowning, though the   46
ship were no stronger than a nutshell and as leaky as an   47
unstanched wench.

BOATSWAIN   Lay her ahold, ahold! Set her two courses!   49
Off to sea again! Lay her off!   50
Enter Mariners wet.

MARINERS   All lost! To prayers, to prayers! All lost!
[Exeunt.]

BOATSWAIN   What, must our mouths be cold?

GONZALO
The king and prince at prayers! Let's assist them,
For our case is as theirs.

SEBASTIAN   I am out of patience.

ANTONIO
We are merely cheated of our lives by drunkards.   55
This wide-chopped rascal – would thou mightst lie   56
drowning
The washing of ten tides!   57

GONZALO   He'll be hanged yet,
Though every drop of water swear against it
And gape at wid'st to glut him.   59
A confused noise within: "Mercy on us! –
We split, we split! – Farewell, my wife and children! – 60
Farewell, brother! – We split, we split, we split!"
[Exit Boatswain.]

ANTONIO
Let's all sink with th' king.

SEBASTIAN   Let's take leave of him.
Exit [with Antonio].

---

46 *warrant . . . for* guarantee . . . against   47–48 *as leaky . . . wench* (a joke
probably about a woman menstruating without using any absorbent
padding, but possibly about her being unsatisfied though sexually aroused)
49 *Lay her ahold* bring the ship close to the wind (this would hold it away
from the rocks but would require more sail); *two courses* foresail and mainsail
50 *Lay her off* take the ship out to sea   55 *merely* completely   56 *wide-chopped* wide-jawed   57 *ten tides* (pirates were hanged on shore and left
until three tides washed over them)   59 *glut* swallow

GONZALO   Now would I give a thousand furlongs of sea
64 for an acre of barren ground – long heath, brown furze,
anything. The wills above be done, but I would fain die
a dry death.   *Exit.*

                                *

∾ I.2 *Enter Prospero and Miranda.*

MIRANDA
1   If by your art, my dearest father, you have
     Put the wild waters in this roar, allay them.
     The sky, it seems, would pour down stinking pitch
4   But that the sea, mounting to th' welkin's cheek,
     Dashes the fire out. O, I have suffered
6   With those that I saw suffer! A brave vessel
     (Who had no doubt some noble creature in her)
     Dashed all to pieces! O, the cry did knock
     Against my very heart! Poor souls, they perished!
10   Had I been any god of power, I would
11   Have sunk the sea within the earth or ere
     It should the good ship so have swallowed and
13   The fraughting souls within her.
PROSPERO   Be collected.
14   No more amazement. Tell your piteous heart
     There's no harm done.
MIRANDA   O, woe the day!
PROSPERO   No harm.
     I have done nothing but in care of thee,
     Of thee my dear one, thee my daughter, who
     Art ignorant of what thou art, naught knowing
     Of whence I am; nor that I am more better

---

64 *long heath, brown furze* heather and gorse
    I.2 The island   1 *art* magic, skill   4 *welkin's cheek* sky's face   6 *brave*
fine, noble, handsome (and so elsewhere throughout the play)   11 *or ere* before   13 *fraughting* forming the cargo; *collected* composed   14 *amazement*
fear, wonder; *piteous* pitying

Than Prospero, master of a full poor cell,   20
And thy no greater father.

MIRANDA   More to know
Did never meddle with my thoughts.   22

PROSPERO   'Tis time
I should inform thee farther. Lend thy hand
And pluck my magic garment from me. *[Miranda*
helps Prospero to take off his magic robe.] So,
Lie there, my art. Wipe thou thine eyes; have comfort.   25
The direful spectacle of the wrack, which touched
The very virtue of compassion in thee,
I have with such provision in mine art   28
So safely ordered that there is no soul —
No, not so much perdition as an hair   30
Betid to any creature in the vessel   31
Which thou heard'st cry, which thou saw'st sink. Sit
   down;
For thou must now know farther.

MIRANDA   You have often
Begun to tell me what I am; but stopped
And left me to a bootless inquisition,   35
Concluding, "Stay: not yet."

PROSPERO   The hour's now come;
The very minute bids thee ope thine ear.
Obey, and be attentive. Canst thou remember
A time before we came unto this cell?
I do not think thou canst, for then thou wast not   40
Out three years old.   41

MIRANDA   Certainly, sir, I can.

PROSPERO
By what? By any other house or person?
Of anything the image tell me that   43
Hath kept with thy remembrance.

---

20 *cell* a hermit's or poor person's dwelling or small cottage (not a prison cell)
22 *meddle* mingle, interfere   **25** *art* i.e., his robe   **28** *provision* foresight   **30**
perdition loss   **31** *Betid* happened   **35** *bootless inquisition* fruitless inquiry
41 *Out* fully   **43** *tell me* i.e., describe for me

MIRANDA   'Tis far off,
And rather like a dream than an assurance
46   That my remembrance warrants. Had I not
Four or five women once that tended me?

PROSPERO
Thou hadst, and more, Miranda. But how is it
That this lives in thy mind? What seest thou else
50   In the dark backward and abysm of time?
If thou rememb'rest aught ere thou cam'st here,
How thou cam'st here thou mayst.

MIRANDA   But that I do not.

PROSPERO
Twelve year since, Miranda, twelve year since,
Thy father was the Duke of Milan and
A prince of power.

MIRANDA   Sir, are not you my father?

PROSPERO
56   Thy mother was a piece of virtue, and
She said thou wast my daughter; and thy father
58   Was Duke of Milan; and his only heir
59   And princess – no worse issued.

MIRANDA .   O the heavens!
60   What foul play had we that we came from thence?
Or blessèd was't we did?

PROSPERO   Both, both, my girl!
By foul play, as thou say'st, were we heaved thence,
63   But blessedly holp hither.

MIRANDA   O, my heart bleeds
64   To think o' th' teen that I have turned you to,
65   Which is from my remembrance! Please you, farther.

PROSPERO
My brother and thy uncle, called Antonio –
I pray thee mark me – that a brother should

---

46 *remembrance warrants* memory guarantees 50 *backward* past; *abysm*
abyss 56 *piece* masterpiece 58 *Milan* (stressed on first syllable) 59 *no
worse issued* no meaner in descent 63 *blessedly holp* providentially helped
64 *teen* trouble; *turned you to* put you in mind of 65 *from* out of

Be so perfidious! – he whom next thyself
Of all the world I loved, and to him put   69
The manage of my state, as at that time   70
Through all the signories it was the first   71
And Prospero the prime duke, being so reputed
In dignity, and for the liberal arts
Without a parallel; those being all my study,
The government I cast upon my brother
And to my state grew stranger, being transported
And rapt in secret studies. Thy false uncle –
Dost thou attend me?
MIRANDA   Sir, most heedfully.
PROSPERO
Being once perfected how to grant suits,   79
How to deny them, who t' advance, and who   80
To trash for overtopping, new-created   81
The creatures that were mine, I say, or changed 'em,   82
Or else new-formed 'em; having both the key   83
Of officer and office, set all hearts i' th' state
To what tune pleased his ear, that now he was
The ivy which had hid my princely trunk
And sucked my verdure out on't. Thou attend'st not?   87
MIRANDA
O, good sir, I do.
PROSPERO   I pray thee mark me.
I thus neglecting worldly ends, all dedicated
To closeness, and the bettering of my mind   90
With that which, but by being so retired,   91
O'erprized all popular rate, in my false brother   92
Awaked an evil nature, and my trust,
Like a good parent, did beget of him   94

69–70 *put . . . state* entrusted the administration of my dukedom 71 *sig-nories* states of northern Italy 79 *Being . . . perfected* having once mastered the skills of 81 *trash for overtopping* check, as hounds, for going too fast 82 *or* either 83 *key* (used with pun on its musical sense, leading to the metaphor of *tune*) 87 *verdure* sap, vitality 90 *closeness* seclusion 91 *but* merely 92 *O'erprized . . . rate* exceeded the people's understanding 94 *good parent* (alluding to the same proverb cited by Miranda in l. 120)

A falsehood in its contrary as great
As my trust was, which had indeed no limit,
97   A confidence sans bound. He being thus lorded,
98   Not only with what my revenue yielded
But what my power might else exact, like one
100 Who having unto truth, by telling of it,
Made such a sinner of his memory
102 To credit his own lie, he did believe
103 He was indeed the duke, out o' th' substitution
And executing th' outward face of royalty
With all prerogative. Hence his ambition growing –
Dost thou hear?

MIRANDA   Your tale, sir, would cure deafness.

PROSPERO
To have no screen between this part he played
And him he played it for, he needs will be
109 Absolute Milan. Me (poor man) my library
110 Was dukedom large enough. Of temporal royalties
111 He thinks me now incapable; confederates
112 (So dry he was for sway) with th' King of Naples
To give him annual tribute, do him homage,
Subject his coronet to his crown, and bend
115 The dukedom yet unbowed (alas, poor Milan!)
To most ignoble stooping.

MIRANDA   O the heavens!

PROSPERO
117 Mark his condition, and th' event; then tell me
If this might be a brother.

MIRANDA   I should sin
To think but nobly of my grandmother.
120 Good wombs have borne bad sons.

---

97 *sans bound* unlimited   97–99 *He . . . exact* (the sense is that Antonio had
the prerogatives as well as the income of the duke)   98 *revenue* (accent second syllable)   100 *it* i.e., the lie   102 *To* as to   103 *out* as a result   109 *Absolute Milan* Duke of Milan completely; *Me* as for me   110 *temporal royalties*
practical rule   111 *confederates* joins in league with   112 *dry* thirsty, eager
115 *yet* hitherto   117 *condition* pact; *event* outcome

PROSPERO   Now the condition.
  This King of Naples, being an enemy
To me inveterate, hearkens my brother's suit;
Which was, that he, in lieu o' th' premises   123
Of homage and I know not how much tribute,
Should presently extirpate me and mine   125
Out of the dukedom and confer fair Milan,
With all the honors, on my brother. Whereon,
A treacherous army levied, one midnight
Fated to th' purpose, did Antonio open   129
The gates of Milan; and i' th' dead of darkness,   130
The ministers for th' purpose hurried thence   131
Me and thy crying self.
MIRANDA   Alack, for pity!
  I, not rememb'ring how I cried out then,
Will cry it o'er again; it is a hint   134
That wrings mine eyes to't.
PROSPERO   Hear a little further,
  And then I'll bring thee to the present business
Which now's upon's; without the which this story
Were most impertinent.   138
MIRANDA   Wherefore did they not
  That hour destroy us?
PROSPERO   Well demanded, wench.
  My tale provokes that question. Dear, they durst not,   140
So dear the love my people bore me; nor set
A mark so bloody on the business; but
With colors fairer painted their foul ends.
In few, they hurried us aboard a bark,   144
Bore us some leagues to sea; where they prepared
A rotten carcass of a butt, not rigged,   146
Nor tackle, sail, nor mast; the very rats

---

123 *in lieu o' th' premises* in return for the guarantees   **125** *presently* immediately; *extirpate* remove (accent second syllable)   **129** *Fated* chosen by fate   **131** *ministers* agents   **134** *hint* occasion   **138** *impertinent* irrelevant   **144** *few* few words   **146** *butt* tub

Instinctively have quit it. There they hoist us,
To cry to th' sea that roared to us; to sigh
150 To th' winds, whose pity, sighing back again,
Did us but loving wrong.

MIRANDA   Alack, what trouble
Was I then to you!

PROSPERO   O, a cherubin
Thou wast that did preserve me! Thou didst smile,
Infusèd with a fortitude from heaven,
155 When I have decked the sea with drops full salt,
Under my burden groaned: which raised in me
157 An undergoing stomach, to bear up
Against what should ensue.

MIRANDA   How came we ashore?

PROSPERO
By providence divine.
160 Some food we had, and some fresh water, that
A noble Neapolitan, Gonzalo,
Out of his charity, who being then appointed
Master of this design, did give us, with
Rich garments, linens, stuffs, and necessaries
165 Which since have steaded much. So, of his gentleness,
Knowing I loved my books, he furnished me
From mine own library with volumes that
I prize above my dukedom.

MIRANDA   Would I might
But ever see that man!

PROSPERO   Now I arise.
170 Sit still, and hear the last of our sea sorrow.
Here in this island we arrived; and here
172 Have I, thy schoolmaster, made thee more profit
173 Than other princes can, that have more time
For vainer hours, and tutors not so careful.

---

155 *decked* adorned   157 *undergoing stomach* determination to endure
165 *steaded* been of use   172 *more profit* profit more   173 *princes* (royal
children of either gender)

MIRANDA

    Heavens thank you for't! And now I pray you, sir –

    For still 'tis beating in my mind – your reason

    For raising this sea storm?

PROSPERO   Know thus far forth.

    By accident most strange, bountiful Fortune

    (Now, my dear lady) hath mine enemies

    Brought to this shore; and by my prescience   *180*

    I find my zenith doth depend upon   181

    A most auspicious star, whose influence

    If now I court not, but omit, my fortunes   183

    Will ever after droop. Here cease more questions.

    Thou art inclined to sleep. 'Tis a good dullness,   185

    And give it way. I know thou canst not choose.

       [Miranda sleeps.]

    Come away, servant, come! I am ready now.   187

    Approach, my Ariel: come!   188

       Enter Ariel.

ARIEL

    All hail, great master! Grave sir, hail! I come

    To answer thy best pleasure; be't to fly,   *190*

    To swim, to dive into the fire, to ride

    On the curled clouds. To thy strong bidding task

    Ariel and all his quality.   193

PROSPERO   Hast thou, spirit,

    Performed to point the tempest that I bade thee?   194

ARIEL

    To every article.

    I boarded the king's ship: now on the beak,   196

    Now in the waist, the deck, in every cabin,   197

    I flamed amazement: sometime I'd divide   198

    And burn in many places; on the topmast,

---

181 *zenith* apex of fortune   183 *omit* neglect   185 *dullness* drowsiness
187 *Come away* come here   188 *Ariel* (in Hebrew, it means "Lion of God";
a common name for a spirit in magical texts)   193 *quality* cohorts (Ariel is
leader of a band of elemental spirits)   194 *to point* in detail   196 *beak* prow
197 *waist* amidships; *deck* poop   198 *flamed amazement* struck terror by appearing as (Saint Elmo's) fire

200 The yards, and bowsprit would I flame distinctly,
Then meet and join. Jove's lightnings, the precursors
O' th' dreadful thunderclaps, more momentary
And sight-outrunning were not. The fire and cracks
Of sulphurous roaring the most mighty Neptune
Seem to besiege and make his bold waves tremble;
Yea, his dread trident shake.

PROSPERO   My brave spirit!
207 Who was so firm, so constant, that this coil
Would not infect his reason?

ARIEL   Not a soul
209 But felt a fever of the mad and played
210 Some tricks of desperation. All but mariners
Plunged in the foaming brine and quit the vessel,
212 Then all afire with me; the king's son Ferdinand,
213 With hair upstaring (then like reeds, not hair),
Was the first man that leapt, cried "Hell is empty,
And all the devils are here!"

PROSPERO   Why, that's my spirit!
But was not this nigh shore?

ARIEL   Close by, my master.

PROSPERO
But are they, Ariel, safe?

ARIEL   Not a hair perished.
218 On their sustaining garments not a blemish,
But fresher than before; and as thou bad'st me,
220 In troops I have dispersed them 'bout the isle.
The king's son have I landed by himself,
Whom I left cooling of the air with sighs
In an odd angle of the isle, and sitting,
224 His arms in this sad knot.

---

200 *distinctly* in different places   **207** *coil* uproar   **209** *of the mad* such as
madmen have   **212** *afire with me* (refers either to the vessel or, possibly, to
Ferdinand, depending on the punctuation; F suggests the latter)   **213** *upstaring* standing on end   **218** *sustaining* buoying them up in the water   **224**
this (illustrated by a gesture)

PROSPERO   Of the king's ship
  The mariners say how thou hast disposed,
  And all the rest o' th' fleet.
ARIEL   Safely in harbor
  Is the king's ship; in the deep nook where once
  Thou call'dst me up at midnight to fetch dew
  From the still-vexed Bermudas, there she's hid;   229
  The mariners all under hatches stowed,   230
  Who, with a charm joined to their suffered labor,   231
  I have left asleep; and for the rest o' th' fleet,
  Which I dispersed, they all have met again,
  And are upon the Mediterranean float   234
  Bound sadly home for Naples,
  Supposing that they saw the king's ship wracked
  And his great person perish.
PROSPERO   Ariel, thy charge
  Exactly is performed; but there's more work.
  What is the time o' th' day?   239
ARIEL   Past the midseason.
PROSPERO
  At least two glasses. The time 'twixt six and now   240
  Must by us both be spent most preciously.
ARIEL
  Is there more toil? Since thou dost give me pains,
  Let me remember thee what thou hast promised,   243
  Which is not yet performed me.
PROSPERO   How now? moody?
  What is't thou canst demand?
ARIEL   My liberty.
PROSPERO   Before the time be out? No more!   246
ARIEL   I prithee,
  Remember I have done thee worthy service,
  Told thee no lies, made no mistakes, served

---

229 *still-vexed* always stormy   231 *suffered* undergone   234 *float* sea   239
midseason noon   240 *glasses* hours   243 *remember* remind   246 *time* period
of service

Without or grudge or grumblings. Thou did promise
250   To bate me a full year.

PROSPERO   Dost thou forget
From what a torment I did free thee?

ARIEL   No.

PROSPERO
Thou dost; and think'st it much to tread the ooze
Of the salt deep,
To run upon the sharp wind of the North,
255   To do me business in the veins o' th' earth
256   When it is baked with frost.

ARIEL   I do not, sir.

PROSPERO
Thou liest, malignant thing! Hast thou forgot
258   The foul witch Sycorax, who with age and envy
Was grown into a hoop? Hast thou forgot her?

ARIEL
260   No, sir.

PROSPERO   Thou hast. Where was she born? Speak!
Tell me!

ARIEL
261   Sir, in Argier.

PROSPERO   O, was she so? I must
Once in a month recount what thou hast been,
Which thou forget'st. This damned witch Sycorax,
For mischiefs manifold, and sorceries terrible
To enter human hearing, from Argier,
266   Thou know'st, was banished. For one thing she did
They would not take her life. Is not this true?

ARIEL
Ay, sir.

---

250 *bate me* shorten my term of service   255 *veins* streams   256 *baked*
hardened   258 *Sycorax* (name not found elsewhere; usually connected with
Greek *sys*, sow, and *korax*, which means both "raven" – cf. l. 322 – and
"curved," hence perhaps *hoop*); *envy* malice   261 *Argier* Algiers   266 *one thing*
she did (being pregnant, her sentence was commuted from death to exile)

PROSPERO
   This blue-eyed hag was hither brought with child   269
   And here was left by th' sailors. Thou, my slave,   270
   As thou report'st thyself, wast then her servant;
   And, for thou wast a spirit too delicate
   To act her earthy and abhorred commands,
   Refusing her grand hests, she did confine thee,   274
   By help of her more potent ministers,
   And in her most unmitigable rage,
   Into a cloven pine; within which rift
   Imprisoned thou didst painfully remain
   A dozen years; within which space she died
   And left thee there, where thou didst vent thy groans   280
   As fast as mill wheels strike. Then was this island   281
   (Save for the son that she did litter here,
   A freckled whelp, hag-born) not honored with
   A human shape.
ARIEL   Yes, Caliban her son.
PROSPERO
   Dull thing, I say so: he, that Caliban
   Whom now I keep in service. Thou best know'st
   What torment I did find thee in: thy groans
   Did make wolves howl and penetrate the breasts   288
   Of ever-angry bears. It was a torment
   To lay upon the damned, which Sycorax   290
   Could not again undo. It was mine art,
   When I arrived and heard thee, that made gape
   The pine, and let thee out.
ARIEL   I thank thee, master.
PROSPERO
   If thou more murmur'st, I will rend an oak
   And peg thee in his knotty entrails till   295
   Thou hast howled away twelve winters.   296

---

269 *blue-eyed* (blue eyelids were held to be a sign of pregnancy) **274** *hests* commands **281** *mill wheels* the blades of waterwheels **288** *penetrate the breasts* (and arouse sympathy in) **295** *his* its **296** *twelve* (the same length of time that Ariel has been released)

ARIEL   Pardon, master.
297   I will be correspondent to command
298   And do my spriting gently.
PROSPERO   Do so; and after two days
      I will discharge thee.
ARIEL   That's my noble master!
300   What shall I do? Say what? What shall I do?
PROSPERO
      Go make thyself like a nymph o' th' sea. Be subject
      To no sight but thine and mine, invisible
      To every eyeball else. Go take this shape
      And hither come in't. Go! Hence with diligence!
                                         Exit [Ariel].
      Awake, dear heart, awake! Thou hast slept well.
      Awake!
MIRANDA   The strangeness of your story put
      Heaviness in me.
PROSPERO   Shake it off. Come on.
      We'll visit Caliban, my slave, who never
      Yields us kind answer.
MIRANDA   'Tis a villain, sir,
310   I do not love to look on.
PROSPERO   But as 'tis,
311   We cannot miss him: he does make our fire,
      Fetch in our wood, and serves in offices
      That profit us. What, ho! slave! Caliban!
      Thou earth, thou! Speak!
CALIBAN   *[Within]*   There's wood enough within.
PROSPERO
      Come forth, I say! There's other business for thee.
316   Come, thou tortoise! When?
            Enter Ariel like a water nymph.
317   Fine apparition! My quaint Ariel,
      Hark in thine ear.

_____

297 *correspondent* obedient 298 *spriting gently* office as a spirit graciously
311 *miss* do without 316 *When* (expression of impatience) 317 *quaint* ingenious

ARIEL   My lord, it shall be done.   *Exit.*

PROSPERO

Thou poisonous slave, got by the devil himself
Upon thy wicked dam, come forth!   *320*
   Enter Caliban.

CALIBAN

As wicked dew as e'er my mother brushed   *321*
With raven's feather from unwholesome fen
Drop on you both! A southwest blow on ye   *323*
And blister you all o'er!

PROSPERO

For this, be sure, tonight thou shalt have cramps,
Side stitches that shall pen thy breath up; urchins   *326*
Shall, for that vast of night that they may work,   *327*
All exercise on thee; thou shalt be pinched
As thick as honeycomb, each pinch more stinging
Than bees that made 'em.   *330*

CALIBAN   I must eat my dinner.

This island's mine by Sycorax my mother,
Which thou tak'st from me. When thou cam'st first,
Thou strok'st me and made much of me; wouldst give me
Water with berries in't; and teach me how
To name the bigger light, and how the less,
That burn by day and night; and then I loved thee
And showed thee all the qualities o' th' isle,   *337*
The fresh springs, brine pits, barren place and fertile.
Cursèd be I that did so! All the charms   *339*
Of Sycorax – toads, beetles, bats, light on you!   *340*
For I am all the subjects that you have,
Which first was mine own king; and here you sty me
In this hard rock, whiles you do keep from me
The rest o' th' island.

---

321 *dew* (often used in magic; see l. 228)   323 *southwest* (a wind linked to
warm, damp, and unhealthy weather)   326 *urchins* goblins in the shape of
hedgehogs   327 *vast* void; *that they may work* (referring to the belief that
malignant spirits had power only during darkness)   337 *qualities* resources
339 *charms* spells

PROSPERO   Thou most lying slave,
345   Whom stripes may move, not kindness! I have used thee
       (Filth as thou art) with humane care, and lodged thee
       In mine own cell till thou didst seek to violate
       The honor of my child.

CALIBAN
       O ho, O ho! Would't had been done!
350   Thou didst prevent me; I had peopled else
       This isle with Calibans.

351   MIRANDA   Abhorrèd slave,
       Which any print of goodness wilt not take,
       Being capable of all ill! I pitied thee,
       Took pains to make thee speak, taught thee each hour
       One thing or other: when thou didst not, savage,
       Know thine own meaning, but wouldst gabble like
357   A thing most brutish, I endowed thy purposes
358   With words that made them known. But thy vile race,
       Though thou didst learn, had that in't which good
          natures
360   Could not abide to be with; therefore wast thou
       Deservedly confined into this rock,
       Who hadst deserved more than a prison.

CALIBAN
       You taught me language, and my profit on't
364   Is, I know how to curse. The red plague rid you
       For learning me your language!

PROSPERO   Hagseed, hence!
366   Fetch us in fuel; and be quick, thou'rt best,
       To answer other business. Shrug'st thou, malice?
       If thou neglect'st or dost unwillingly
369   What I command, I'll rack thee with old cramps,
370   Fill all thy bones with aches, make thee roar
       That beasts shall tremble at thy din.

---

345 *stripes* lashes 351 *MIRANDA* (so F; early editors often gave the speech to
Prospero) 357 *purposes* meanings 358 *race* nature 364 *red plague* plague,
producing bleeding or sores; *rid* destroy 366 *thou'rt best* you'd be well ad-
vised 369 *old* i.e., such as old people have 370 *aches* (pronounced
"aitches")

CALIBAN   No, pray thee.
  [Aside]
  I must obey. His art is of such pow'r
  It would control my dam's god, Setebos,
  And make a vassal of him.
PROSPERO   So, slave; hence!
                                        Exit Caliban.
  Enter Ferdinand; and Ariel (invisible), playing and
  singing.
ARIEL   *[Sings.]*
            Come unto these yellow sands,
              And then take hands.
            Curtsied when you have and kissed,
              The wild waves whist,   378
            Foot it featly here and there;   379
            And, sweet sprites, the burden bear.   380
              Hark, hark!
Burden, dispersedly.   Bow-wow.   382
            The watchdogs bark.
Burden, dispersedly.   Bow-wow.
            Hark, hark! I hear
            The strain of strutting chanticleer
            Cry cock-a-diddle-dow.
FERDINAND
  Where should this music be? I' th' air or th' earth?
  It sounds no more; and sure it waits upon
  Some god o' th' island. Sitting on a bank,   390
  Weeping again the king my father's wrack,
  This music crept by me upon the waters,
  Allaying both their fury and my passion   393
  With its sweet air. Thence I have followed it,

---

378 *whist* being hushed   379 *featly* nimbly   382 *Burden* refrain (sung by
spirits); *dispersedly* (1) not in unison, (2) from several directions   393 *pas-*
sion lamentation

Or it hath drawn me rather; but 'tis gone.
No, it begins again.

ARIEL   *[Sings.]*

    Full fathom five thy father lies;
      Of his bones are coral made;
    Those are pearls that were his eyes;

400
      Nothing of him that doth fade
      But doth suffer a sea change
    Into something rich and strange.
    Sea nymphs hourly ring his knell:

Burden.   Ding-dong.
    Hark! now I hear them – Ding-dong bell.

FERDINAND

406   The ditty does remember my drowned father.
    This is no mortal business, nor no sound
408   That the earth owes. I hear it now above me.

PROSPERO   *[To Miranda]*

409   The fringèd curtains of thine eye advance
410   And say what thou seest yond.

MIRANDA   What is't? a spirit?
    Lord, how it looks about! Believe me, sir,
    It carries a brave form. But 'tis a spirit.

PROSPERO

    No, wench: it eats, and sleeps, and hath such senses
    As we have, such. This gallant which thou seest
415   Was in the wrack; and, but he's something stained
416   With grief (that's beauty's canker), thou mightst call him
    A goodly person. He hath lost his fellows
    And strays about to find 'em.

MIRANDA   I might call him
    A thing divine; for nothing natural
420   I ever saw so noble.

---

406 *remember* commemorate **408** *owes* owns **409** *advance* raise **415**
stained disfigured **416** *canker* consuming disease

PROSPERO   *[Aside]*   It goes on, I see,
  As my soul prompts it. Spirit, fine spirit, I'll free thee   421
  Within two days for this.   422
FERDINAND   Most sure, the goddess
  On whom these airs attend! Vouchsafe my prayer   423
  May know if you remain upon this island,   424
  And that you will some good instruction give
  How I may bear me here. My prime request,   426
  Which I do last pronounce, is (O you wonder!)   427
  If you be maid or no?   428
MIRANDA   No wonder, sir,
  But certainly a maid.
FERDINAND   My language? Heavens!
  I am the best of them that speak this speech,   430
  Were I but where 'tis spoken.
PROSPERO   How? the best?
  What wert thou if the King of Naples heard thee?
FERDINAND
  A single thing, as I am now, that wonders   433
  To hear thee speak of Naples. He does hear me;
  And that he does I weep. Myself am Naples,   435
  Who with mine eyes, never since at ebb, beheld   436
  The king my father wracked.
MIRANDA   Alack, for mercy!
FERDINAND
  Yes, faith, and all his lords, the Duke of Milan
  And his brave son being twain.   439
PROSPERO   *[Aside]*   The Duke of Milan
  And his more braver daughter could control thee,   440
  If now 'twere fit to do't. At the first sight

---

420 *It* my plan **421** *prompts* would like **422** *Most sure* this is certainly
423 *airs* songs **424** *remain* dwell **426** *bear me* conduct myself **427** *wonder* (unknowingly, Ferdinand puns on Miranda's name – i.e., a woman who
must be wondered at) **428** *maid* a single girl (as opposed to a goddess or a
married woman) **433** *A single thing* just one person **435** *Naples* King of
Naples **436** *never . . . ebb* crying nonstop ever since **439** *son* (Antonio's
son is not mentioned elsewhere) **440** *control* refute

442   They have changed eyes. Delicate Ariel,
       I'll set thee free for this. – A word, good sir.
444   I fear you have done yourself some wrong. A word!

MIRANDA
       Why speaks my father so ungently? This
       Is the third man that e'er I saw; the first
       That e'er I sighed for. Pity move my father
       To be inclined my way!

FERDINAND   O, if a virgin,
       And your affection not gone forth, I'll make you
450   The Queen of Naples.

PROSPERO   Soft, sir! one word more.
         [Aside]
       They are both in either's pow'rs. But this swift business
452   I must uneasy make, lest too light winning
       Make the prize light. – One word more! I charge thee
       That thou attend me. Thou dost here usurp
455   The name thou ow'st not, and hast put thyself
       Upon this island as a spy, to win it
       From me, the lord on't.

FERDINAND   No, as I am a man!

MIRANDA
       There's nothing ill can dwell in such a temple.
       If the ill spirit have so fair a house,
460   Good things will strive to dwell with't.

PROSPERO   Follow me. –
       Speak not you for him; he's a traitor. – Come!
       I'll manacle thy neck and feet together;
       Seawater shalt thou drink; thy food shall be
       The fresh-brook mussels, withered roots, and husks
       Wherein the acorn cradled. Follow!

FERDINAND   No.
466   I will resist such entertainment till
       Mine enemy has more pow'r.

---

442 *changed eyes* exchanged love looks   444 *done . . . wrong* told a lie   452
light (Prospero puns on the word's meanings: easy, cheap, promiscuous)
455 *ow'st* ownest   466 *entertainment* treatment

He draws, and is charmed from moving.

MIRANDA   O dear father,
Make not too rash a trial of him, for   468
He's gentle, and not fearful.   469
PROSPERO   What, I say,
My foot my tutor? – Put thy sword up, traitor!   470
Who mak'st a show but dar'st not strike, thy conscience
Is so possessed with guilt. Come, from thy ward!   472
For I can here disarm thee with this stick
And make thy weapon drop.
MIRANDA   Beseech you, father!
PROSPERO
Hence! Hang not on my garments.
MIRANDA   Sir, have pity.
I'll be his surety.
PROSPERO   Silence! One word more
Shall make me chide thee, if not hate thee. What,
An advocate for an impostor? Hush!
Thou think'st there is no more such shapes as he,
Having seen but him and Caliban. Foolish wench!   480
To th' most of men this is a Caliban,
And they to him are angels.   482
MIRANDA   My affections
Are then most humble. I have no ambition
To see a goodlier man.
PROSPERO   Come on, obey!
Thy nerves are in their infancy again   485
And have no vigor in them.
FERDINAND   So they are.
My spirits, as in a dream, are all bound up.
My father's loss, the weakness which I feel,
The wrack of all my friends, nor this man's threats
To whom I am subdued, are but light to me,   490
Might I but through my prison once a day

---

468 *trial* judgment   **469** *gentle* noble; *fearful* cowardly   **470** *My ... tutor*
i.e., instructed by my underling   **472** *ward* fighting posture   **482** *affections*
inclinations   **485** *nerves* sinews, tendons

Behold this maid. All corners else o' th' earth
Let liberty make use of. Space enough
Have I in such a prison.

PROSPERO   *[Aside]*   It works. *[To Ferdinand]* Come on.
         [To Ariel]
495   Thou hast done well, fine Ariel!
         [To Ferdinand]   Follow me.
         [To Ariel]
      Hark what thou else shalt do me.

MIRANDA   Be of comfort.
      My father's of a better nature, sir,
      Than he appears by speech. This is unwonted
      Which now came from him.

PROSPERO   Thou shalt be as free
500   As mountain winds; but then exactly do
      All points of my command.

ARIEL   To th' syllable.

PROSPERO
      Come, follow. *[To Miranda]* Speak not for him.

                                                Exeunt.

                          *

~ **II.1** *Enter Alonso, Sebastian, Antonio, Gonzalo,*
      Adrian, Francisco.

GONZALO
      Beseech you, sir, be merry. You have cause
      (So have we all) of joy; for our escape
3   Is much beyond our loss. Our hint of woe
      Is common: every day some sailor's wife,
5   The master of some merchant, and the merchant,

495–96 (which parts of these lines are to Ferdinand and which to Ariel are
arguable editorial decisions) **500** *then* till then
    II.1 s.d. (F adds *"and others"* after *"Francisco"* and puts *"etc."* at the be-
ginning of III.3, but these extra attendants are missing in the entry at V.1.57,
where they would disturb the pattern; it is more consistent to delete them
here and at the start of III.3 as well) **3** *hint* occasion **5** *master of some merchant* master of a merchant ship; *the merchant* the owner of the ship

Have just our theme of woe; but for the miracle,
I mean our preservation, few in millions
Can speak like us. Then wisely, good sir, weigh
Our sorrow with our comfort.

ALONSO   Prithee peace.

SEBASTIAN   He receives comfort like cold porridge.   10

ANTONIO   The visitor will not give him o'er so.   11

SEBASTIAN   Look, he's winding up the watch of his wit;
by and by it will strike.

GONZALO   Sir –

SEBASTIAN   One. Tell.   15

GONZALO
   – when every grief is entertained
That's offered, comes to th' entertainer –   17

SEBASTIAN   A dollar.

GONZALO   Dolor comes to him, indeed. You have   19
spoken truer than you purposed.   20

SEBASTIAN   You have taken it wiselier than I meant you
should.

GONZALO   Therefore, my lord –

ANTONIO   Fie, what a spendthrift is he of his tongue!   24

ALONSO   I prithee spare.

GONZALO   Well, I have done. But yet –

SEBASTIAN   He will be talking.

ANTONIO   Which, of he or Adrian, for a good wager, first
begins to crow?

SEBASTIAN   The old cock.   30

ANTONIO   The cock'rel.   31

SEBASTIAN   Done! The wager?

ANTONIO   A laughter.   33

SEBASTIAN   A match!

ADRIAN   Though this island seem to be desert –

ANTONIO   Ha, ha, ha!

---

10 *porridge* (pun on "peace" [pease])   11 *visitor* churchman who comforts the
sick; *give him o'er* let him alone   15 *Tell* count   17 *That's* that which is; *entertainer* (taken by Sebastian to mean "innkeeper")   19 *Dolor* grief (with pun
on "dollar," a Continental coin)   24 *spendthrift* (Antonio labors the pun)   30
old cock i.e., Gonzalo   31 *cock'rel* i.e., Adrian   33 *laughter* the winner laughs

SEBASTIAN   So, you're paid.

ADRIAN   Uninhabitable and almost inaccessible –

SEBASTIAN   Yet –

40 ADRIAN   Yet –

ANTONIO   He could not miss't.

ADRIAN   It must needs be of subtle, tender, and delicate
43   temperance.

44 ANTONIO   Temperance was a delicate wench.

45 SEBASTIAN   Ay, and a subtle, as he most learnedly deliv-
ered.

ADRIAN   The air breathes upon us here most sweetly.

SEBASTIAN   As if it had lungs, and rotten ones.

ANTONIO   Or as 'twere perfumed by a fen.

50 GONZALO   Here is everything advantageous to life.

ANTONIO   True; save means to live.

SEBASTIAN   Of that there's none, or little.

53 GONZALO   How lush and lusty the grass looks! how
green!

ANTONIO   The ground indeed is tawny.

56 SEBASTIAN   With an eye of green in't.

ANTONIO   He misses not much.

SEBASTIAN   No; he doth but mistake the truth totally.

GONZALO   But the rarity of it is – which is indeed almost
60   beyond credit –

61 SEBASTIAN   As many vouched rarities are.

GONZALO   That our garments, being, as they were,
drenched in the sea, hold, notwithstanding, their fresh-
ness and gloss, being rather new-dyed than stained with
salt water.

ANTONIO   If but one of his pockets could speak, would it
not say he lies?

SEBASTIAN   Ay, or very falsely pocket up his report.

---

43 *temperance* climate   44 *Temperance* (a girl's name); *delicate* given to pleasure   45 *subtle* crafty, expert in sex   53 *lush* tender, soft   56 *eye* spot   61
vouched rarities wonders guaranteed to be true

GONZALO   Methinks our garments are now as fresh as
when we put them on first in Afric, at the marriage of   *70*
the king's fair daughter Claribel to the King of Tunis.

SEBASTIAN   'Twas a sweet marriage, and we prosper well
in our return.

ADRIAN   Tunis was never graced before with such a
paragon to their queen.   *75*

GONZALO   Not since widow Dido's time.   *76*

ANTONIO   Widow? A pox o' that! How came that
"widow" in? Widow Dido!

SEBASTIAN   What if he had said "widower Aeneas" too?
Good Lord, how you take it!   *80*

ADRIAN   "Widow Dido," said you? You make me study
of that. She was of Carthage, not of Tunis.

GONZALO   This Tunis, sir, was Carthage.

ADRIAN   Carthage?

GONZALO   I assure you, Carthage.

ANTONIO   His word is more than the miraculous harp.   *86*

SEBASTIAN   He hath raised the wall and houses too.

ANTONIO   What impossible matter will he make easy
next?

SEBASTIAN   I think he will carry this island home in his   *90*
pocket and give it his son for an apple.

ANTONIO   And, sowing the kernels of it in the sea, bring
forth more islands.

GONZALO   Ay!   *94*

ANTONIO   Why, in good time.

---

75 *to* for **76** *widow Dido* (Dido was the widow of Sychaeus; Aeneas was a
widower, having lost his wife in the fall of Troy. Antonio may be mockingly
suggesting that she was only a widow – i.e., a woman abandoned by her
lover [not necessarily a woman whose husband had died], because abandoned by Aeneas [who had not married her], but the comment has not been
convincingly explained.) **86** *miraculous harp* (of Amphion, which raised the
walls of Thebes; Tunis and Carthage were near each other, but not the same
city, though Tunis became the name for the region where Carthage was)
94 *Ay* (F reads "I" and might indicate that Gonzalo is starting a new sentence, "I – ," which Antonio interrupts)

GONZALO   Sir, we were talking that our garments seem
now as fresh as when we were at Tunis at the marriage
of your daughter, who is now queen.

ANTONIO   And the rarest that e'er came there.

100 SEBASTIAN   Bate, I beseech you, widow Dido.

ANTONIO   O, widow Dido? Ay, widow Dido!

GONZALO   Is not, sir, my doublet as fresh as the first day
103 I wore it? I mean, in a sort.

ANTONIO   That "sort" was well fished for.

GONZALO   When I wore it at your daughter's marriage.

ALONSO
You cram these words into mine ears against
107 The stomach of my sense. Would I had never
Married my daughter there! for, coming thence,
109 My son is lost; and, in my rate, she too,
110 Who is so far from Italy removed
I ne'er again shall see her. O thou mine heir
Of Naples and of Milan, what strange fish
Hath made his meal on thee?

FRANCISCO   Sir, he may live.
I saw him beat the surges under him
And ride upon their backs. He trod the water,
Whose enmity he flung aside, and breasted
The surge most swol'n that met him. His bold head
'Bove the contentious waves he kept, and oared
Himself with his good arms in lusty stroke
120 To th' shore, that o'er his wave-worn basis bowed,
As stooping to relieve him. I not doubt
He came alive to land.

ALONSO   No, no, he's gone.

SEBASTIAN
Sir, you may thank yourself for this great loss,
That would not bless our Europe with your daughter,

---

100 *Bate* except   103 *in a sort* i.e., comparatively   107 *stomach . . . sense*
i.e., temper of my perception   109 *rate* estimation   120 *his* its; *basis* foot of
the cliff

But rather loose her to an African,
Where she, at least, is banished from your eye
Who hath cause to wet the grief on't.
ALONSO   Prithee peace.
SEBASTIAN
    You were kneeled to and importuned otherwise
    By all of us; and the fair soul herself   129
    Weighed, between loathness and obedience, at   130
    Which end o' th' beam should bow. We have lost your
        son,
    I fear, forever. Milan and Naples have
    Moe widows in them of this business' making   133
    Than we bring men to comfort them:
    The fault's your own.   135
ALONSO   So is the dear'st o' th' loss.
GONZALO
    My Lord Sebastian,
    The truth you speak doth lack some gentleness,
    And time to speak it in. You rub the sore
    When you should bring the plaster.
SEBASTIAN   Very well.
ANTONIO
    And most chirurgeonly.   140
GONZALO
    It is foul weather in us all, good sir,
    When you are cloudy.
SEBASTIAN   Foul weather?
ANTONIO   Very foul.
GONZALO
    Had I plantation of this isle, my lord –   143
ANTONIO
    He'd sow't with nettle seed.   144

129–31 *the fair . . . bow* (the sense is that Claribel hated the marriage, and
only obedience to her father turned the scale)   133 *Moe* more   135 *dear'st*
heaviest   140 *chirurgeonly* like a surgeon   143 *plantation* colonization
(taken by Antonio in its other sense)

SEBASTIAN   Or docks, or mallows.

GONZALO
  And were the king on't, what would I do?

SEBASTIAN
  Scape being drunk for want of wine.

GONZALO
147 I' th' commonwealth I would by contraries
148 Execute all things; for no kind of traffic
     Would I admit; no name of magistrate;
150 Letters should not be known; riches, poverty,
151 And use of service, none; contract, succession,
152 Bourn, bound of land, tilth, vineyard, none;
     No use of metal, corn, or wine, or oil;
     No occupation; all men idle, all;
155 And women too, but innocent and pure;
     No sovereignty.

SEBASTIAN   Yet he would be king on't.

ANTONIO   The latter end of his commonwealth forgets
  the beginning.

GONZALO
159 All things in common nature should produce
160 Without sweat or endeavor. Treason, felony,
161 Sword, pike, knife, gun, or need of any engine
     Would I not have; but nature should bring forth,
163 Of it own kind, all foison, all abundance,
     To feed my innocent people.

SEBASTIAN   No marrying 'mong his subjects?

ANTONIO   None, man, all idle – whores and knaves.

GONZALO
  I would with such perfection govern, sir,
  T' excel the golden age.

SEBASTIAN   Save his majesty!

---

144 *docks . . . mallows* (antidotes to nettle stings)   147 *by contraries* in contrast to usual customs   148 *traffic* trade   151 *use of service* having a servant
class; *succession* inheritance   152 *Bourn* limits of private property   155 (in-
verting the proverb "Idleness begets lust")   159 *in common* for communal
use   161 *engine* weapon   163 *it* its; *foison* abundance

ANTONIO
    Long live Gonzalo!
GONZALO   And – do you mark me, sir?
ALONSO
    Prithee no more. Thou dost talk nothing to me.   170
GONZALO   I do well believe your highness; and did it to
    minister occasion to these gentlemen, who are of such   172
    sensible and nimble lungs that they always use to laugh   173
    at nothing.
ANTONIO   'Twas you we laughed at.
GONZALO   Who in this kind of merry fooling am noth-
    ing to you: so you may continue, and laugh at nothing
    still.
ANTONIO   What a blow was there given!
SEBASTIAN   An it had not fall'n flatlong.   180
GONZALO   You are gentlemen of brave mettle; you
    would lift the moon out of her sphere if she would con-
    tinue in it five weeks without changing.
        Enter Ariel [invisible,] playing solemn music.
SEBASTIAN   We would so, and then go a-batfowling.   184
ANTONIO   Nay, good my lord, be not angry.
GONZALO   No, I warrant you: I will not adventure my   186
    discretion so weakly. Will you laugh me asleep, for I am
    very heavy?
ANTONIO   Go sleep, and hear us.   189
        [All sleep except Alonso, Sebastian, and Antonio.]
ALONSO
    What, all so soon asleep? I wish mine eyes   190
    Would, with themselves, shut up my thoughts. I find
    They are inclined to do so.
SEBASTIAN   Please you, sir,
    Do not omit the heavy offer of it.   193

---

172 *minister occasion* afford opportunity   **173** *sensible* sensitive   **180** *An* if;
flatlong struck with the flat of a sword, so harmlessly   **184** *a-batfowling*
hunting birds with sticks ("bats") at night (using the moon for a lantern)
186 *adventure* risk (Gonzalo is saying, very politely, that their wit is too fee-
ble for him to take offense at it)   **189** *hear us* listen to us laughing   **193**
omit neglect; *heavy offer* opportunity its heaviness affords

It seldom visits sorrow; when it doth,
It is a comforter.
ANTONIO   We two, my lord,
Will guard your person while you take your rest,
And watch your safety.
ALONSO   Thank you. Wondrous heavy.
                    [Alonso sleeps. Exit Ariel.]

SEBASTIAN
What a strange drowsiness possesses them!
ANTONIO
It is the quality o' th' climate.
SEBASTIAN   Why
200   Doth it not then our eyelids sink? I find not
Myself disposed to sleep.
ANTONIO   Nor I: my spirits are nimble.
They fell together all, as by consent.
They dropped as by a thunderstroke. What might,
Worthy Sebastian – O, what might? – No more!
And yet methinks I see it in thy face,
206   What thou shouldst be. Th' occasion speaks thee, and
My strong imagination sees a crown
Dropping upon thy head.
SEBASTIAN   What? Art thou waking?
ANTONIO
Do you not hear me speak?
SEBASTIAN   I do; and surely
210   It is a sleepy language, and thou speak'st
Out of thy sleep. What is it thou didst say?
This is a strange repose, to be asleep
With eyes wide open; standing, speaking, moving,
And yet so fast asleep.
ANTONIO   Noble Sebastian,
215   Thou let'st thy fortune sleep – die, rather; wink'st
Whiles thou art waking.
SEBASTIAN   Thou dost snore distinctly;
There's meaning in thy snores.

---

206 *speaks* speaks to, summons   **215** *wink'st* you sleep

ANTONIO
    I am more serious than my custom. You
    Must be so too, if heed me; which to do
    Trebles thee o'er.   220
SEBASTIAN   Well, I am standing water.
ANTONIO
    I'll teach you how to flow.
SEBASTIAN   Do so. To ebb
    Hereditary sloth instructs me.   222
ANTONIO   O,
    If you but knew how you the purpose cherish   223
    Whiles thus you mock it! how, in stripping it,
    You more invest it! Ebbing men indeed   225
    (Most often) do so near the bottom run
    By their own fear or sloth.
SEBASTIAN   Prithee say on.
    The setting of thine eye and cheek proclaim
    A matter from thee; and a birth, indeed,   229
    Which throes thee much to yield.   230
ANTONIO   Thus, sir:
    Although this lord of weak remembrance, this   231
    Who shall be of as little memory   232
    When he is earthed, hath here almost persuaded   233
    (For he's a spirit of persuasion, only
    Professes to persuade) the king his son's alive,   235
    'Tis as impossible that he's undrowned
    As he that sleeps here swims.
SEBASTIAN   I have no hope
    That he's undrowned
ANTONIO   O, out of that no hope
    What great hope have you! No hope that way is
    Another way so high a hope that even   240

------

220 *Trebles thee o'er* increases your status threefold; *standing water* at slack
tide 222 *Hereditary sloth* natural laziness 223 *cherish* enrich 225 *invest*
clothe 229 *A matter* something important 230 *throes thee much* costs you
much pain, like a birth 231 *remembrance* memory 232 *of . . . memory* as
little remembered 233 *earthed* buried 235 *Professes* has the function

241   Ambition cannot pierce a wink beyond,
242   But doubt discovery there. Will you grant with me
       That Ferdinand is drowned?
SEBASTIAN   He's gone.
ANTONIO   Then tell me,
       Who's the next heir of Naples?
SEBASTIAN   Claribel.
ANTONIO
       She that is Queen of Tunis; she that dwells
246   Ten leagues beyond man's life; she that from Naples
247   Can have no note, unless the sun were post –
       The man i' th' moon's too slow – till new-born chins
       Be rough and razorable; she that from whom
250   We all were sea-swallowed, though some cast again,
       And, by that destiny, to perform an act
       Whereof what's past is prologue, what to come,
253   In yours and my discharge.
SEBASTIAN   What stuff is this? How say you?
       'Tis true my brother's daughter's Queen of Tunis;
       So is she heir of Naples; 'twixt which regions
       There is some space.
ANTONIO   A space whose ev'ry cubit
       Seems to cry out "How shall that Claribel
258   Measure us back to Naples? Keep in Tunis,
       And let Sebastian wake!" Say this were death
260   That now hath seized them, why, they were no worse
       Than now they are. There be that can rule Naples
       As well as he that sleeps; lords that can prate
       As amply and unnecessarily
       As this Gonzalo; I myself could make
265   A chough of as deep chat. O, that you bore

---

241 *wink* glimpse   242 *doubt discovery there* is uncertain of seeing accurately
246 *Ten . . . life* i.e., thirty miles from nowhere   247 *note* communication;
post messenger   250 *cast* thrown up (with a suggestion of its theatrical
meaning, which introduces the next metaphor)   253 *discharge* performance
258 *us* i.e., the cubits   265 *chough* jackdaw (a bird sometimes taught to
speak)

The mind that I do! What a sleep were this
For your advancement! Do you understand me?
SEBASTIAN
Methinks I do.   268
ANTONIO   And how does your content
Tender your own good fortune?
SEBASTIAN   I remember
You did supplant your brother Prospero.   270
ANTONIO   True.
And look how well my garments sit upon me,
Much feater than before. My brother's servants   272
Were then my fellows; now they are my men.   273
SEBASTIAN
But, for your conscience –
ANTONIO
Ay, sir, where lies that? If 'twere a kibe,   275
'Twould put me to my slipper; but I feel not   276
This deity in my bosom. Twenty consciences
That stand 'twixt me and Milan, candied be they   278
And melt, ere they molest! Here lies your brother,
No better than the earth he lies upon   280
If he were that which now he's like – that's dead;
Whom I with this obedient steel (three inches of it)
Can lay to bed forever; whiles you, doing thus,
To the perpetual wink for aye might put   284
This ancient morsel, this Sir Prudence, who
Should not upbraid our course. For all the rest,
They'll take suggestion as a cat laps milk;
They'll tell the clock to any business that   288
We say befits the hour.
SEBASTIAN   Thy case, dear friend,
Shall be my precedent. As thou got'st Milan,   290

268–69 *content Tender* inclination estimate   272 *feater* more stylishly   273
fellows equals; *men* servants   275 *kibe* chilblain   276 *put me to* make me
wear   278 *candied* frozen   284 *wink* sleep   288 *tell the clock* answer appropriately

I'll come by Naples. Draw thy sword. One stroke
Shall free thee from the tribute which thou payest,
And I the king shall love thee.

ANTONIO   Draw together;
And when I rear my hand, do you the like,
To fall it on Gonzalo.
        [They draw.]
SEBASTIAN   O, but one word!
        Enter Ariel [invisible], with music and song.

ARIEL
My master through his art foresees the danger
That you, his friend, are in, and sends me forth
(For else his project dies) to keep them living.
        Sings in Gonzalo's ear.
                While you here do snoring lie,
                Open-eyed conspiracy
                    His time doth take.
                If of life you keep a care,
                Shake off slumber and beware.
                    Awake, awake!

ANTONIO
Then let us both be sudden.
GONZALO   *[Wakes.]*   Now good angels
Preserve the king!
ALONSO
Why, how now? – Ho, awake! – Why are you drawn?
Wherefore this ghastly looking?
GONZALO   What's the matter?
SEBASTIAN
Whiles we stood here securing your repose,
Even now, we heard a hollow burst of bellowing
Like bulls, or rather lions. Did't not wake you?
It struck mine ear most terribly.
ALONSO   I heard nothing.

---

295 *fall it* let it fall   **295 s.d.** *with music* either "with an instrument" or "accompanied by musicians"   **309** *securing* keeping watch over

ANTONIO
  O, 'twas a din to fright a monster's ear,
  To make an earthquake! Sure it was the roar
  Of a whole herd of lions.
ALONSO   Heard you this, Gonzalo?
GONZALO
  Upon mine honor, sir, I heard a humming,
  And that a strange one too, which did awake me.
  I shaked you, sir, and cried. As mine eyes opened,
  I saw their weapons drawn. There was a noise,
  That's verily. 'Tis best we stand upon our guard,   320
  Or that we quit this place. Let's draw our weapons.
ALONSO
  Lead off this ground, and let's make further search
  For my poor son.
GONZALO   Heavens keep him from these beasts!
  For he is sure i' th' island.
ALONSO   Lead away.
ARIEL
  Prospero my lord shall know what I have done.
  So, king, go safely on to seek thy son.   *Exeunt.*

                        *

∾ **II.2** *Enter Caliban with a burden of wood.*

CALIBAN
  All the infections that the sun sucks up
  From bogs, fens, flats, on Prosper fall, and make him
  By inchmeal a disease! *(A noise of thunder heard.)* His   3
    spirits hear me,
  And yet I needs must curse. But they'll nor pinch,   4
  Fright me with urchin shows, pitch me i' th' mire,   5
  Nor lead me, like a firebrand, in the dark   6

II.2 **3** *By inchmeal* inch by inch **3 s.d.** (in F this appears at the head of the
scene) **4** *nor* neither **5** *urchin shows* apparitions in the form of hedgehogs
6 *like a firebrand* like a torch

Out of my way, unless he bid 'em; but
For every trifle are they set upon me;
9   Sometime like apes that mow and chatter at me,
10   And after bite me; then like hedgehogs which
Lie tumbling in my barefoot way and mount
Their pricks at my footfall; sometime am I
All wound with adders, who with cloven tongues
Do hiss me into madness.

     Enter Trinculo.   Lo, now, lo!
Here comes a spirit of his, and to torment me
For bringing wood in slowly. I'll fall flat.
Perchance he will not mind me.

     [Lies down and covers himself with his cloak.]

18 TRINCULO   Here's neither bush nor shrub to bear off any
weather at all, and another storm brewing: I hear it sing
20   i' th' wind. Yond same black cloud, yond huge one,
21   looks like a foul bombard that would shed his liquor. If
it should thunder as it did before, I know not where to
hide my head. Yond same cloud cannot choose but fall
by pailfuls. What have we here? a man or a fish? dead or
alive? A fish: he smells like a fish; a very ancient and
26   fishlike smell; a kind of not of the newest Poor John. A
strange fish! Were I in England now, as once I was, and
28   had but this fish painted, not a holiday fool there but
would give a piece of silver. There would this monster
30   make a man: any strange beast there makes a man.
31   When they will not give a doit to relieve a lame beggar,
32   they will lay out ten to see a dead Indian. Legged like a
man! and his fins like arms! Warm, o' my troth! I do
now let loose my opinion, hold it no longer: this is no
fish, but an islander, that hath lately suffered by a thun-
derbolt. *[Thunder.]* Alas, the storm is come again! My

---

9 *mow* make faces   18 *bear off* ward off   21 *bombard* leather bottle; *his* its
26 *Poor John* dried, salted fish   28 *painted* i.e., on a signboard outside a
booth at a fair   30 *make a man* (also with sense of "make a man's fortune")
31 *doit* small coin   32 *a dead Indian* (natives of the New World had often
been brought back and displayed, to the substantial profit of the exhibitor
but usually causing the native to die from disease)

best way is to creep under his gaberdine: there is no 37
other shelter hereabout. Misery acquaints a man with
strange bedfellows. I will here shroud till the dregs of
the storm be past.   40
   [Creeps under Caliban's garment.]
   Enter Stephano, singing [with a bottle in his hand].
STEPHANO   I shall no more to sea, to sea;
            Here shall I die ashore.

This is a very scurvy tune to sing at a man's funeral.
Well, here's my comfort.
   Drinks.

   The master, the swabber, the boatswain, and I,   45
      The gunner, and his mate,
   Loved Mall, Meg, and Marian, and Margery,
      But none of us cared for Kate.
      For she had a tongue with a tang,
      Would cry to a sailor "Go hang!"   50
   She loved not the savor of tar nor of pitch;
   Yet a tailor might scratch her where'er she did itch.   52
      Then to sea, boys, and let her go hang!

This is a scurvy tune too; but here's my comfort.
   Drinks.
CALIBAN   Do not torment me! O!
STEPHANO   What's the matter? Have we devils here? Do
you put tricks upon's with savages and men of Ind, ha? 57
I have not scaped drowning to be afeard now of your
four legs; for it hath been said, "As proper a man as ever
went on four legs cannot make him give ground"; and 60
it shall be said so again, while Stephano breathes at nos-
trils.

---

37 *gaberdine* cloak   45 *swabber* seaman who cleans the decks   52 *a tailor* (a cliché for a man lacking virility); *scratch* have sex with   57 *men of Ind* inhabitants of the West Indies   60 *four legs* (the proverb's usual form is, of course, "two legs")

CALIBAN The spirit torments me. O!

STEPHANO This is some monster of the isle, with four
legs, who hath got, as I take it, an ague. Where the devil
should he learn our language? I will give him some re-
lief, if it be but for that. If I can recover him, and keep
him tame, and get to Naples with him, he's a present
69 for any emperor that ever trod on neat's leather.

70 CALIBAN Do not torment me, prithee; I'll bring my
wood home faster.

STEPHANO He's in his fit now and does not talk after the
wisest. He shall taste of my bottle: if he have never
drunk wine afore, it will go near to remove his fit. If I
75 can recover him and keep him tame, I will not take too
much for him; he shall pay for him that hath him, and
that soundly.

CALIBAN Thou dost me yet but little hurt. Thou wilt
79 anon; I know it by thy trembling. Now Prosper works
80 upon thee.

STEPHANO Come on your ways; open your mouth: here
82 is that which will give language to you, cat. Open your
mouth. This will shake your shaking, I can tell you,
and that soundly. *[Gives Caliban drink.]* You cannot tell
85 who's your friend. Open your chaps again.

TRINCULO I should know that voice. It should be – but
he is drowned; and these are devils. O, defend me!

88 STEPHANO Four legs and two voices – a most delicate
monster! His forward voice now is to speak well of his
90 friend; his backward voice is to utter foul speeches and
to detract. If all the wine in my bottle will recover him,
I will help his ague. Come! *[Gives drink.]* Amen! I will
pour some in thy other mouth.

TRINCULO Stephano!

---

69 *neat's leather* cowhide **75–76** *not take too much* i.e., take all I can get **79**
anon soon **82** *cat* (alluding to the proverb "Liquor will make a cat talk")
85 *chaps* jaws **88** *delicate* exquisitely made

STEPHANO   Doth thy other mouth call me? Mercy,
mercy! This is a devil, and no monster. I will leave him;
I have no long spoon.   97

TRINCULO   Stephano! If thou beest Stephano, touch me
and speak to me; for I am Trinculo – be not afeard –
thy good friend Trinculo.   100

STEPHANO   If thou beest Trinculo, come forth. I'll pull
thee by the lesser legs. If any be Trinculo's legs, these are
they. *[Pulls him out from under Caliban's cloak.]* Thou
art very Trinculo indeed: how cam'st thou to be the
siege of this mooncalf? Can he vent Trinculos?   105

TRINCULO   I took him to be killed with a thunderstroke. But art thou not drowned, Stephano? I hope
now thou art not drowned. Is the storm overblown? I
hid me under the dead mooncalf's gaberdine for fear of
the storm. And art thou living, Stephano? O Stephano, 110
two Neapolitans scaped!

STEPHANO   Prithee do not turn me about: my stomach is
not constant.

CALIBAN   *[Aside]*
These be fine things, an if they be not sprites.   114
That's a brave god and bears celestial liquor.
I will kneel to him.

STEPHANO   How didst thou scape? How cam'st thou
hither? Swear by this bottle how thou cam'st hither. I
escaped upon a butt of sack which the sailors heaved   119
o'erboard, by this bottle, which I made of the bark of a 120
tree with mine own hands since I was cast ashore.

CALIBAN   I'll swear upon that bottle to be thy true subject, for the liquor is not earthly.

STEPHANO   Here! Swear then how thou escapedst.

TRINCULO   Swum ashore, man, like a duck. I can swim
like a duck, I'll be sworn.

---

97 *spoon* (alluding to the proverb "He who sups with the devil must have a
long spoon")   105 *siege* excrement; *mooncalf* monstrosity; *vent* shit   114 *an
if* if   119 *butt of sack* barrel of Spanish white wine (often sherry)

127   STEPHANO   Here, kiss the book. *[Gives him drink.]*
Though thou canst swim like a duck, thou art made
129   like a goose.

130   TRINCULO   O Stephano, hast any more of this?

STEPHANO   The whole butt, man: my cellar is in a rock
by th' seaside, where my wine is hid. How now, mooncalf? How does thine ague?

CALIBAN   Hast thou not dropped from heaven?

STEPHANO   Out o' th' moon, I do assure thee. I was the
136   Man i' th' Moon when time was.

CALIBAN
I have seen thee in her, and I do adore thee.
My mistress showed me thee, and thy dog, and thy
bush.

STEPHANO   Come, swear to that; kiss the book. I will
140   furnish it anon with new contents. Swear.
    [Caliban drinks.]

TRINCULO   By this good light, this is a very shallow
monster! I afeard of him? A very weak monster! The
Man i' th' Moon? A most poor credulous monster! –
Well drawn, monster, in good sooth!

CALIBAN
I'll show thee every fertile inch o' th' island;
And I will kiss thy foot. I prithee be my god.

TRINCULO   By this light, a most perfidious and drunken
monster! When's god's asleep, he'll rob his bottle.

CALIBAN
I'll kiss thy foot. I'll swear myself thy subject.

150   STEPHANO   Come on then. Down, and swear!

TRINCULO   I shall laugh myself to death at this puppy-
headed monster. A most scurvy monster! I could find
in my heart to beat him –

STEPHANO   Come, kiss.

TRINCULO   But that poor monster's in drink. An abom-
inable monster!

---

127 *book* i.e., bottle   129 *like a goose* (Trinculo is standing unsteadily)   **136**
when time was once upon a time

CALIBAN
   I'll show thee the best springs; I'll pluck thee berries;
   I'll fish for thee, and get thee wood enough.
   A plague upon the tyrant that I serve!
   I'll bear him no more sticks, but follow thee,   *160*
   Thou wondrous man.
TRINCULO   A most ridiculous monster, to make a won-
   der of a poor drunkard!
CALIBAN
   I prithee let me bring thee where crabs grow;   *164*
   And I with my long nails will dig thee pignuts,   *165*
   Show thee a jay's nest, and instruct thee how
   To snare the nimble marmoset; I'll bring thee   *167*
   To clust'ring filberts, and sometimes I'll get thee   *168*
   Young scamels from the rock. Wilt thou go with me?   *169*
STEPHANO   I prithee now, lead the way without any more   *170*
   talking. Trinculo, the king and all our company else being
   drowned, we will inherit here. *[To Caliban]* Here, bear   *172*
   my bottle. Fellow Trinculo, we'll fill him by and by again.   *173*
CALIBAN   *[Sings drunkenly.]* Farewell, master; farewell,
   farewell!
TRINCULO   A howling monster! a drunken monster!
CALIBAN
       No more dams I'll make for fish,
          Nor fetch in firing
          At requiring,
       Nor scrape trenchering, nor wash dish.   *180*
         'Ban, 'Ban, Ca – Caliban
         Has a new master: get a new man.   *182*
  Freedom, high-day! high-day, freedom! freedom, high-
  day, freedom!
STEPHANO   O brave monster! lead the way.   *Exeunt.*

---

164 *crabs* crab apples (probably not shellfish)   165 *pignuts* earthnuts   167
marmoset a small monkey (said to be edible)   168 *filberts* hazelnuts   169
scamels (unexplained, but clearly either a shellfish or a rock-nesting bird; perhaps a misprint for "seamels," sea mews)   172 *inherit* take possession   173
by and by soon   180 *trenchering* trenchers, wooden plates   182 *get a new
man* (addressed to Prospero)

*

∾ **III.1** *Enter Ferdinand, bearing a log.*

FERDINAND

1   There be some sports are painful, and their labor
     Delight in them sets off; some kinds of baseness
3   Are nobly undergone, and most poor matters
     Point to rich ends. This my mean task
     Would be as heavy to me as odious, but
6   The mistress which I serve quickens what's dead
     And makes my labors pleasures. O, she is
     Ten times more gentle than her father's crabbed;
     And he's composed of harshness! I must remove
10   Some thousands of these logs and pile them up,
11   Upon a sore injunction. My sweet mistress
     Weeps when she sees me work, and says such baseness
     Had never like executor. I forget;
     But these sweet thoughts do even refresh my labors
15   Most busiest, when I do it.
          Enter Miranda; and Prospero [behind, unseen].
     MIRANDA   Alas, now pray you
     Work not so hard! I would the lightning had
     Burnt up those logs that you are enjoined to pile!
     Pray set it down and rest you. When this burns,
19   'Twill weep for having wearied you. My father
20   Is hard at study: pray now rest yourself.
     He's safe for these three hours.
     FERDINAND   O most dear mistress,
     The sun will set before I shall discharge
     What I must strive to do.

III.1 1 *painful* strenuous   **1–2** *their labor . . . sets off* either "the pleasure balances the hard work they require" or "the hard work adds luster to the pleasure"   **3** *matters* affairs   **6** *quickens* brings to life   **11** *sore injunction* harsh command   **15** *busilest* most busily (this is a famous textual crux; "busilest" is the best solution proposed)   **19** *weep* i.e., exude resin

MIRANDA   If you'll sit down,
  I'll bear your logs the while. Pray give me that:
  I'll carry it to the pile.
FERDINAND   No, precious creature:
  I had rather crack my sinews, break my back,
  Than you should such dishonor undergo
  While I sit lazy by.
MIRANDA   It would become me
  As well as it does you; and I should do it
  With much more ease; for my good will is to it,   30
  And yours it is against.
PROSPERO *[Aside]*   Poor worm, thou art infected!
  This visitation shows it.   32
MIRANDA   You look wearily.
FERDINAND
  No, noble mistress: 'tis fresh morning with me
  When you are by at night. I do beseech you,
  Chiefly that I might set it in my prayers,
  What is your name?
MIRANDA   Miranda. O my father,
  I have broke your hest to say so!   37
FERDINAND   Admired Miranda!
  Indeed the top of admiration, worth   38
  What's dearest to the world! Full many a lady
  I have eyed with best regard, and many a time   40
  Th' harmony of their tongues hath into bondage
  Brought my too diligent ear; for several virtues   42
  Have I liked several women; never any
  With so full soul but some defect in her   44
  Did quarrel with the noblest grace she owed,   45
  And put it to the foil. But you, O you,   46
  So perfect and so peerless, are created
  Of every creature's best.

---

32 *visitation* (1) visit to the sick, (2) attack of plague (in the metaphor of *infected*) 37 *hest* command 38 *admiration* wonder, astonishment (punning on Miranda's name; cf. I.2.427) 40 *best regard* highest approval 42 *several* different 44 *With . . . soul* i.e., so wholeheartedly 45 *owed* owned 46 *foil* (1) overthrow, (2) contrast

MIRANDA   I do not know
One of my sex; no woman's face remember,
50   Save, from my glass, mine own; nor have I seen
More that I may call men than you, good friend,
52   And my dear father. How features are abroad
53   I am skill-less of; but, by my modesty
(The jewel in my dower), I would not wish
Any companion in the world but you;
Nor can imagination form a shape,
57   Besides yourself, to like of. But I prattle
Something too wildly, and my father's precepts
59   I therein do forget.
FERDINAND   I am, in my condition,
60   A prince, Miranda; I do think, a king
(I would not so), and would no more endure
This wooden slavery than to suffer
63   The flesh fly blow my mouth. Hear my soul speak!
The very instant that I saw you, did
My heart fly to your service; there resides,
To make me slave to it; and for your sake
Am I this patient log-man.
MIRANDA   Do you love me?
FERDINAND
O heaven, O earth, bear witness to this sound,
69   And crown what I profess with kind event
70   If I speak true! if hollowly, invert
What best is boded me to mischief! I,
Beyond all limit of what else i' th' world,
Do love, prize, honor you.
MIRANDA   I am a fool
To weep at what I am glad of.
PROSPERO *[Aside]*   Fair encounter
Of two most rare affections! Heavens rain grace
On that which breeds between 'em!

---

52 *abroad* elsewhere   53 *skill-less* ignorant; *modesty* virginity   57 *like of*
compare to   59 *condition* situation in the world   63 *flesh fly* fly that breeds
in dead flesh; *blow* deposit its eggs in   69 *kind event* favorable outcome

FERDINAND   Wherefore weep you?
MIRANDA
    At mine unworthiness, that dare not offer
    What I desire to give, and much less take
    What I shall die to want. But this is trifling;   79
    And all the more it seeks to hide itself,   80
    The bigger bulk it shows. Hence, bashful cunning,   81
    And prompt me, plain and holy innocence!
    I am your wife, if you will marry me;
    If not, I'll die your maid. To be your fellow   84
    You may deny me; but I'll be your servant,
    Whether you will or no.
FERDINAND   My mistress, dearest,
    And I thus humble ever.
MIRANDA   My husband then?
FERDINAND
    Ay, with a heart as willing
    As bondage e'er of freedom. Here's my hand.   89
MIRANDA
    And mine, with my heart in't; and now farewell   90
    Till half an hour hence.
FERDINAND   A thousand thousand!
              Exeunt [Ferdinand and Miranda severally].
PROSPERO
    So glad of this as they I cannot be,
    Who are surprised withal; but my rejoicing   93
    At nothing can be more. I'll to my book;
    For yet ere suppertime must I perform
    Much business appertaining.   *Exit.* 96
                          *

---

79 *want* lack 80–81 *all the ... shows* (the image is of a secret pregnancy)
81 *bashful cunning* a pretense of shyness 84 *maid* servant, virgin; *fellow*
equal 89 *of freedom* i.e., to win freedom 93 *surprised withal* taken unaware
by it 96 *appertaining* relevant

∾ **III.2** *Enter Caliban, Stephano, and Trinculo.*

1 STEPHANO   Tell not me! When the butt is out, we will
2   drink water; not a drop before. Therefore bear up and
    board 'em! Servant monster, drink to me.

TRINCULO   Servant monster? The folly of this island!
    They say there's but five upon this isle: we are three of
    them. If th' other two be brained like us, the state
    totters.

STEPHANO   Drink, servant monster, when I bid thee: thy
9   eyes are almost set in thy head.

10 TRINCULO   Where should they be set else? He were a
    brave monster indeed if they were set in his tail.

STEPHANO   My man-monster hath drowned his tongue
    in sack. For my part, the sea cannot drown me. I swam,
14   ere I could recover the shore, five-and-thirty leagues off
    and on, by this light. Thou shalt be my lieutenant,
16   monster, or my standard.

17 TRINCULO   Your lieutenant, if you list; he's no standard.

18 STEPHANO   We'll not run, Monsieur Monster.

19 TRINCULO   Nor go neither; but you'll lie like dogs, and
20   yet say nothing neither.

STEPHANO   Mooncalf, speak once in thy life, if thou beest
    a good mooncalf.

CALIBAN
    How does thy honor? Let me lick thy shoe.
    I'll not serve him; he is not valiant.

TRINCULO   Thou liest, most ignorant monster: I am in
26   case to justle a constable. Why, thou deboshed fish

III.2 1 *butt is out* cask is empty   2–3 *bear . . . 'em* i.e., drink up (Caliban has
almost passed out)   9 *set* fixed drunkenly   14 *recover* reach   16 *standard*
standard-bearer   17 *no standard* i.e., incapable of standing up   18, 19 *run,
lie* (secondary meanings of) make water, excrete   19 *go* walk   26 *case* fit
condition; *justle* jostle; *deboshed* debauched

thou, was there ever man a coward that hath drunk so
much sack as I today? Wilt thou tell a monstrous lie,
being but half a fish and half a monster?

CALIBAN   Lo, how he mocks me! Wilt thou let him, my *30*
lord?

TRINCULO   "Lord" quoth he? That a monster should be
such a natural!   33

CALIBAN

Lo, lo, again! Bite him to death, I prithee.

STEPHANO   Trinculo, keep a good tongue in your head.
If you prove a mutineer – the next tree! The poor monster's my subject, and he shall not suffer indignity.

CALIBAN

I thank my noble lord. Wilt thou be pleased
To hearken once again to the suit I made to thee?

STEPHANO   Marry, will I. Kneel and repeat it; I will *40*
stand, and so shall Trinculo.   41

   Enter Ariel, invisible.

CALIBAN

As I told thee before, I am subject to a tyrant,
A sorcerer, that by his cunning hath
Cheated me of the island.   44

ARIEL   Thou liest.

CALIBAN   *[To Trinculo]*

Thou liest, thou jesting monkey thou!
I would my valiant master would destroy thee.
I do not lie.

STEPHANO   Trinculo, if you trouble him any more in's
tale, by this hand, I will supplant some of your teeth.

TRINCULO   Why, I said nothing.   50

STEPHANO   Mum then, and no more. – Proceed.

CALIBAN

I say by sorcery he got this isle;

---

33 *natural* fool   **41** s.d. *invisible* ("a robe for to go invisible" is in the list of
costumes belonging to the Lord Admiral's Men in the 1590s)   **44** *Thou liest*
(Ariel pretends to be Trinculo here and later in the scene)

From me he got it. If thy greatness will
Revenge it on him – for I know thou dar'st,
55   But this thing dare not –
STEPHANO   That's most certain.
CALIBAN
Thou shalt be lord of it, and I'll serve thee.
STEPHANO
How now shall this be compassed?
59   Canst thou bring me to the party?
CALIBAN
60   Yea, yea, my lord! I'll yield him thee asleep,
Where thou mayst knock a nail into his head.
ARIEL   Thou liest; thou canst not.
CALIBAN
63   What a pied ninny's this! Thou scurvy patch!
I do beseech thy greatness give him blows
And take his bottle from him. When that's gone,
He shall drink naught but brine, for I'll not show him
67   Where the quick freshes are.
STEPHANO   Trinculo, run into no further danger: inter-
rupt the monster one word further and, by this hand, I'll
70   turn my mercy out o' doors and make a stockfish of thee.
TRINCULO   Why, what did I? I did nothing. I'll go far-
ther off.
STEPHANO   Didst thou not say he lied?
ARIEL   Thou liest.
STEPHANO   Do I so? Take thou that! *[Strikes Trinculo.]* As
you like this, give me the lie another time.
TRINCULO   I did not give the lie. Out o' your wits, and
hearing too? A pox o' your bottle! This can sack and
79   drinking do. A murrain on your monster, and the devil
80   take your fingers!
CALIBAN   Ha, ha, ha!

---

55 *this thing* i.e., himself (or perhaps Trinculo)   59 *party* person   63 *pied
ninny* motley fool (Trinculo wears a jester's costume); *patch* clown   67
quick freshes freshwater springs   70 *stockfish* dried cod, prepared by beating
79 *murrain* plague

STEPHANO   Now forward with your tale. *[To Trinculo]*
  Prithee stand further off.
CALIBAN
  Beat him enough. After a little time
  I'll beat him too.
STEPHANO   *[To Trinculo]*
                    Stand farther. *[To Caliban]* Come,
  proceed.
CALIBAN
  Why, as I told thee, 'tis a custom with him
  I' th' afternoon to sleep; there thou mayst brain him,
  Having first seized his books, or with a log
  Batter his skull, or paunch him with a stake,   89
  Or cut his wesand with thy knife. Remember   90
  First to possess his books; for without them
  He's but a sot, as I am, nor hath not   92
  One spirit to command. They all do hate him
  As rootedly as I. Burn but his books.
  He has brave utensils (for so he calls them)   95
  Which, when he has a house, he'll deck withal.
  And that most deeply to consider is
  The beauty of his daughter. He himself
  Calls her a nonpareil. I never saw a woman
  But only Sycorax my dam and she;   100
  But she as far surpasseth Sycorax
  As great'st does least.   102
STEPHANO   Is it so brave a lass?
CALIBAN
  Ay, lord. She will become thy bed, I warrant,
  And bring thee forth brave brood.
STEPHANO   Monster, I will kill this man: his daughter and
  I will be king and queen, save our graces! and Trinculo
  and thyself shall be viceroys. Dost thou like the plot,
  Trinculo?

---

89 *paunch* stab in the belly **90** *wesand* windpipe **92** *sot* fool **95** *utensils*
furnishings **102** *brave* handsome

TRINCULO   Excellent.

110 STEPHANO   Give me thy hand. I am sorry I beat thee; but while thou liv'st, keep a good tongue in thy head.

CALIBAN
Within this half hour he will be asleep.
Wilt thou destroy him then?

STEPHANO   Ay, on mine honor.

ARIEL
This will I tell my master.

CALIBAN
Thou mak'st me merry; I am full of pleasure.

116   Let us be jocund. Will you troll the catch
117   You taught me but whilere?
118 STEPHANO   At thy request, monster, I will do reason, any reason. Come on, Trinculo, let us sing.

> *Sings.*

120   Flout 'em and scout 'em
           And scout 'em and flout 'em!
           Thought is free.

CALIBAN
123   That's not the tune.

> *Ariel plays the tune on a tabor and pipe.*

STEPHANO   What is this same?

TRINCULO   This is the tune of our catch, played by the
126   picture of Nobody.

STEPHANO   If thou beest a man, show thyself in thy like-
128   ness. If thou beest a devil, take't as thou list.

TRINCULO   O, forgive me my sins!

130 STEPHANO   He that dies pays all debts. I defy thee. Mercy upon us!

CALIBAN
Art thou afeard?

STEPHANO   No, monster, not I.

---

116 *troll the catch* sing the round   117 *whilere* just now   118–19 *any reason* anything reasonable   120 *scout* mock   123 **s.d.** *tabor and pipe* a small drum worn at the side and a pipe played one-handed while drumming   126 *Nobody* (referring to pictures of figures with arms and legs but no trunk, used on signs and elsewhere)   128 *take't as thou list* i.e., suit yourself

CALIBAN
    Be not afeard: the isle is full of noises,
    Sounds and sweet airs that give delight and hurt not.
    Sometimes a thousand twangling instruments
    Will hum about mine ears; and sometime voices
    That, if I then had waked after long sleep,
    Will make me sleep again; and then, in dreaming,
    The clouds methought would open and show riches   140
    Ready to drop upon me, that, when I waked,
    I cried to dream again.
STEPHANO This will prove a brave kingdom to me,
    where I shall have my music for nothing.
CALIBAN
    When Prospero is destroyed.
STEPHANO That shall be by and by: I remember the   146
    story.
TRINCULO The sound is going away: let's follow it, and
    after do our work.
STEPHANO Lead, monster; we'll follow. I would I could   150
    see this taborer: he lays it on.
TRINCULO *[To Caliban]* Wilt come? I'll follow
    Stephano.   *Exeunt.*

*

∾ **III.3** *Enter Alonso, Sebastian, Antonio, Gonzalo,*
    Adrian, Francisco, etc.

GONZALO
    By'r Lakin, I can go no further, sir: 1
    My old bones ache: here's a maze trod indeed
    Through forthrights and meanders. By your patience,   3
    I needs must rest me.
ALONSO   Old lord, I cannot blame thee,
    Who am myself attached with weariness   5
    To th' dulling of my spirits. Sit down and rest.

---

146 *by and by* right away
    III.3 1 *By'r Lakin* by our Ladykin (Virgin Mary) **3** *forthrights* straight
paths **5** *attached* seized

Even here I will put off my hope, and keep it
No longer for my flatterer: he is drowned
Whom thus we stray to find; and the sea mocks
10 Our frustrate search on land. Well, let him go.

ANTONIO *[Aside to Sebastian]*
I am right glad that he's so out of hope.
Do not for one repulse forgo the purpose
That you resolved t' effect.

SEBASTIAN *[Aside to Antonio]* The next advantage
14 Will we take throughly.

ANTONIO *[Aside to Sebastian]* Let it be tonight;
For, now they are oppressed with travel, they
Will not nor cannot use such vigilance
17 As when they are fresh.

SEBASTIAN *[Aside to Antonio]* I say tonight. No more.
*Solemn and strange music; and Prospero on the top
(invisible).*

ALONSO
What harmony is this? My good friends, hark!

GONZALO
Marvelous sweet music!
*Enter several strange Shapes, bringing in a banquet;
and dance about it with gentle actions of salutations;
and, inviting the King etc. to eat, they depart.*

ALONSO
20 Give us kind keepers, heavens! What were these?

SEBASTIAN
21 A living drollery. Now I will believe
That there are unicorns; that in Arabia
There is one tree, the phoenix' throne; one phoenix
At this hour reigning there.

ANTONIO   I'll believe both;
25 And what does else want credit, come to me,

---

10 *frustrate* vain 14 *throughly* thoroughly 17 s.d. *on the top* (the topmost
level of the theater, above the gallery over the stage) 20 *kind keepers*
guardian angels 21 *living drollery* puppet show with live figures or comic
pictures come to life 25 *want credit* lack credibility

And I'll be sworn 'tis true. Travelers ne'er did lie,
Though fools at home condemn 'em.
GONZALO   If in Naples
    I should report this now, would they believe me
    If I should say I saw such islanders?
    (For certes these are people of the island)   30
    Who, though they are of monstrous shape, yet note,
    Their manners are more gentle, kind, than of
    Our human generation you shall find
    Many – nay, almost any.
PROSPERO *[Aside]*   Honest lord,
    Thou hast said well; for some of you there present
    Are worse than devils.   36
ALONSO   I cannot too much muse
    Such shapes, such gesture, and such sound, expressing
    (Although they want the use of tongue) a kind
    Of excellent dumb discourse.   39
PROSPERO *[Aside]*   Praise in departing.
FRANCISCO
    They vanished strangely.   40
SEBASTIAN   No matter, since
    They have left their viands behind; for we have   41
        stomachs.
    Will't please you taste of what is here?
ALONSO   Not I.
GONZALO
    Faith, sir, you need not fear. When we were boys,
    Who would believe that there were mountaineers
    Dewlapped like bulls, whose throats had hanging at 'em   45
    Wallets of flesh? or that there were such men
    Whose heads stood in their breasts? which now we find   47

---

30 *certes* certainly **36** *muse* wonder at **39** *Praise in departing* save your
praise for the end **41** *viands* food **45** *Dewlapped* with skin hanging from
the neck (like the supposedly goitrous Swiss mountain dwellers) **47** *in
their breasts* (an ancient traveler's tale; cf. *Othello* I.3.)

48 Each putter-out of five for one will bring us
49 Good warrant of.

ALONSO   I will stand to, and feed;
50 Although my last, no matter, since I feel
    The best is past. Brother, my lord the duke,
52 Stand to, and do as we.

> *Thunder and lightning. Enter Ariel, like a harpy; claps*
> *his wings upon the table; and with a quaint device the*
> *banquet vanishes.*

ARIEL
    You are three men of sin, whom destiny –
54 That hath to instrument this lower world
    And what is in't – the never-surfeited sea
    Hath caused to belch up you, and on this island,
    Where man doth not inhabit, you 'mongst men
    Being most unfit to live, I have made you mad;
    And even with suchlike valor men hang and drown
60 Their proper selves.

> *[Alonso, Sebastian, etc. draw their swords.]*
>   You fools: I and my fellows

    Are ministers of Fate. The elements,
    Of whom your swords are tempered, may as well
    Wound the loud winds, or with bemocked-at stabs
64 Kill the still-closing waters, as diminish
65 One dowl that's in my plume. My fellow ministers
66 Are like invulnerable. If you could hurt,
67 Your swords are now too massy for your strengths
    And will not be uplifted. But remember
    (For that's my business to you) that you three
70 From Milan did supplant good Prospero;
71 Exposed unto the sea, which hath requit it,

---

48 *putter-out . . . one* traveler depositing a sum for insurance in London, to
be repaid fivefold if he returned safely and proved he had gone to his desti-
nation 49 *warrant,* proof; *stand to* set to work 52 **s.d.** *harpy* a creature
with a female face and breasts, and the body, wings, and talons of a bird of
prey (Ariel may have flown in); *quaint* ingenious 54 *to* i.e., as its 64 *still*
constantly 65 *dowl* fiber of feather-down 66 *like* similarly 67 *massy*
heavy 71 *requit* avenged; *it* i.e., the deed

Him and his innocent child; for which foul deed
The pow'rs, delaying, not forgetting, have
Incensed the seas and shores, yea, all the creatures,
Against your peace. Thee of thy son, Alonso,
They have bereft; and do pronounce by me
Ling'ring perdition (worse than any death   77
Can be at once) shall step by step attend
You and your ways; whose wraths to guard you from,
Which here, in this most desolate isle, else falls   80
Upon your heads, is nothing but heart's sorrow   81
And a clear life ensuing.   82
    He vanishes in thunder; then, to soft music, enter the
    Shapes again, and dance with mocks and mows, and
    carrying out the table.

PROSPERO
Bravely the figure of this harpy hast thou
Performed, my Ariel; a grace it had, devouring.   84
Of my instruction hast thou nothing bated   85
In what thou hadst to say. So, with good life   86
And observation strange, my meaner ministers   87
Their several kinds have done. My high charms work,   88
And these, mine enemies, are all knit up
In their distractions: they now are in my pow'r;   90
And in these fits I leave them, while I visit
Young Ferdinand, whom they suppose is drowned,
And his and mine loved darling.   *[Exit above.]*

GONZALO
I' th' name of something holy, sir, why stand you   94
In this strange stare?   95

ALONSO   O, it is monstrous, monstrous!
Methought the billows spoke and told me of it,
The winds did sing it to me, and the thunder,
That deep and dreadful organ pipe, pronounced

---

77 *Ling'ring perdition* slow ruin   81 *heart's sorrow* repentance   82 *clear* innocent; **s.d.** *mocks and mows* grimaces and gestures   84 *devouring* i.e., making the banquet disappear   85 *bated* omitted   86 *good life* realistic acting
87 *observation strange* wonderful attentiveness   88 *several kinds* separate
parts   94 *why* (Gonzalo has not heard Ariel's speech)   95 *it* i.e., my sin

99   The name of Prosper; it did bass my trespass.
100   Therefore my son i' th' ooze is bedded; and
      I'll seek him deeper than e'er plummet sounded
      And with him there lie mudded.   *Exit.*
SEBASTIAN   But one fiend at a time,
103   I'll fight their legions o'er!
ANTONIO   I'll be thy second.
              Exeunt [Sebastian and Antonio].

GONZALO
      All three of them are desperate: their great guilt,
      Like poison given to work a great time after,
      Now 'gins to bite the spirits. I do beseech you,
      That are of suppler joints, follow them swiftly
108   And hinder them from what this ecstasy
      May now provoke them to.
ADRIAN   Follow, I pray you.
              Exeunt omnes.

*

～ IV.1 *Enter Prospero, Ferdinand, and Miranda.*

PROSPERO
1   If I have too austerely punished you,
      Your compensation makes amends; for I
3   Have given you here a third of mine own life,
      Or that for which I live; who once again
      I tender to thy hand. All thy vexations
      Were but my trials of thy love, and thou
7   Hast strangely stood the test. Here, afore heaven,
      I ratify this my rich gift. O Ferdinand,
9   Do not smile at me that I boast her off,
10   For thou shalt find she will outstrip all praise
11   And make it halt behind her.

---

99 *bass* proclaim in deep tones (literally, provide the bass part for) **103** *o'er* one after another **108** *ecstasy* madness

    IV.1 1 *austerely* harshly **3** *third* a very significant part (editors have worried too much what the other two thirds could be) **7** *strangely* in a rare fashion **9** *boast her off* boast about her **11** *halt* limp

FERDINAND   I do believe it
  Against an oracle.   12
PROSPERO
  Then, as my gift, and thine own acquisition
  Worthily purchased, take my daughter. But
  If thou dost break her virgin-knot before
  All sanctimonious ceremonies may   16
  With full and holy rite be ministered,
  No sweet aspersion shall the heavens let fall   18
  To make this contract grow; but barren hate,   19
  Sour-eyed disdain, and discord shall bestrew   20
  The union of your bed with weeds so loathly
  That you shall hate it both. Therefore take heed,
  As Hymen's lamps shall light you.   23
FERDINAND   As I hope
  For quiet days, fair issue, and long life,
  With such love as 'tis now, the murkiest den,
  The most opportune place, the strong'st suggestion   26
  Our worser genius can, shall never melt   27
  Mine honor into lust, to take away
  The edge of that day's celebration
  When I shall think or Phoebus' steeds are foundered   30
  Or Night kept chained below.
PROSPERO   Fairly spoke.
  Sit then and talk with her; she is thine own.
  What, Ariel! My industrious servant, Ariel!
    Enter Ariel.
ARIEL
  What would my potent master? Here I am.
PROSPERO
  Thou and thy meaner fellows your last service
  Did worthily perform; and I must use you

---

12 *Against an oracle* even if an oracle denied it   16 *sanctimonious* holy   18 *aspersion* blessing (like rain on crops)   19 *grow* become fruitful   23 *Hymen's lamps* wedding torches (Hymen was the god of marriage; clear flames indicated a happy marriage, smoky flames a bad one)   26 *opportune* (accent second syllable)   27 *worser genius can* bad angel can make   30 *or . . . foundered* either the sun god's horses are lame

37   In such another trick. Go bring the rabble,
      O'er whom I give thee pow'r, here to this place.
      Incite them to quick motion; for I must
40   Bestow upon the eyes of this young couple
41   Some vanity of mine art; it is my promise,
      And they expect it from me.
ARIEL   Presently?
PROSPERO
      Ay, with a twink.
ARIEL
      Before you can say "Come" and "Go,"
      And breathe twice and cry, "So, so,"
      Each one, tripping on his toe,
47   Will be here with mop and mow.
      Do you love me, master? No?
PROSPERO
      Dearly, my delicate Ariel. Do not approach
50   Till thou dost hear me call.
ARIEL   Well: I conceive.   *Exit.*
PROSPERO
51   Look thou be true: do not give dalliance
      Too much the rein: the strongest oaths are straw
      To th' fire i' th' blood. Be more abstemious,
      Or else good night your vow!
FERDINAND   I warrant you, sir.
      The white cold virgin snow upon my heart
56   Abates the ardor of my liver.
PROSPERO   Well.
57   Now come, my Ariel: bring a corollary
58   Rather than want a spirit. Appear, and pertly!
      [To Ferdinand and Miranda]
59   No tongue! All eyes! Be silent.
      Soft music. Enter Iris.

---

37 *rabble* rank and file   41 *vanity* trifling display   47 *mop and mow* grimaces   50 *conceive* understand   51 *be true* (Prospero appears to have caught
the lovers in an embrace or, if Prospero is overreacting, some contact less ex-
plicitly sexual)   56 *liver* (supposed seat of sexual passion)   57 *corollary* sur-
plus   58 *want* lack; *pertly* briskly   59 **s.d.** *Iris* goddess of the rainbow and
female messenger of the gods

IRIS

    Ceres, most bounteous lady, thy rich leas   60
    Of wheat, rye, barley, fetches, oats, and pease;   61
    Thy turfy mountains, where live nibbling sheep,
    And flat meads thatched with stover, them to keep; 63
    Thy banks with pionèd and twillèd brims,   64
    Which spongy April at thy hest betrims
    To make cold nymphs chaste crowns; and thy broom 66
      groves,
    Whose shadow the dismissèd bachelor loves,
    Being lasslorn; thy pole-clipped vineyard;   68
    And thy sea-marge, sterile and rocky-hard,   69
    Where thou thyself dost air – the queen o' th' sky, 70
    Whose wat'ry arch and messenger am I,
    Bids thee leave these, and with her sovereign grace,
    Here on this grass plot, in this very place,
    To come and sport: her peacocks fly amain.   74
      [Juno's chariot appears above the stage.]
    Approach, rich Ceres, her to entertain.
      Enter Ceres [played by Ariel].

CERES

    Hail, many-colored messenger, that ne'er
    Dost disobey the wife of Jupiter,
    Who, with thy saffron wings, upon my flow'rs
    Diffusest honey drops, refreshing show'rs,
    And with each end of thy blue bow dost crown   *80*
    My bosky acres and my unshrubbed down,   81
    Rich scarf to my proud earth – why hath thy queen
    Summoned me hither to this short-grassed green?

---

60 *leas* meadows   61 *fetches* vetch   63 *stover* winter food for stock   64 *pionèd and twillèd* dug under by the current and protected by woven layers of branches (sometimes emended to "peonied and lilied")   66 *broom groves* clumps of gorse   68 *pole-clipped* pruned; *vineyard* (probably a trisyllable)   69 *sea-marge* shore   70 *queen* i.e., Juno   74 *peacocks* (these were sacred to Juno, as doves were to Venus [l. 94], and drew her chariot)   74 **s.d.** (F has "Juno descended" in the margin by l. 72; "descends" could indicate the appearance of a deity suspended above the stage)   81 *bosky* wooded

IRIS

A contract of true love to celebrate
85 And some donation freely to estate
On the blessed lovers.

CERES   Tell me, heavenly bow,
87 If Venus or her son, as thou dost know,
Do now attend the queen? Since they did plot
89 The means that dusky Dis my daughter got,
90 Her and her blind boy's scandaled company
I have forsworn.

IRIS   Of her society
92 Be not afraid: I met her Deity
93 Cutting the clouds towards Paphos, and her son
Dove-drawn with her. Here thought they to have done
Some wanton charm upon this man and maid,
Whose vows are, that no bed-right shall be paid
Till Hymen's torch be lighted; but in vain.
98 Mars's hot minion is returned again;
99 Her waspish-headed son has broke his arrows,
100 Swears he will shoot no more, but play with sparrows
101 And be a boy right out.

[Juno's chariot descends to the stage.]

CERES   Highest queen of state,
Great Juno, comes; I know her by her gait.

JUNO

103 How does my bounteous sister? Go with me
To bless this twain, that they may prosperous be
And honored in their issue.

They sing.

---

85 *estate* bestow   87 *her son* Cupid (often represented as blind or blind-folded)   89 *means* i.e., the abduction of Proserpine, Ceres' daughter, by Pluto (Dis), god of the lower *(dusky)* world   90 *scandaled* disgraceful   92 *her Deity* i.e., her Divine Majesty   93 *Paphos* (in Cyprus, center of Venus's cult)   98 *Mars's . . . again* the lustful mistress of Mars (Venus) has gone back to where she came from   99 *waspish-headed* spiteful and inclined to sting (with his arrows)   101 *right out* outright   103 *Go with me* (into the chariot?)

JUNO   Honor, riches, marriage blessing,
            Long continuance, and increasing,
            Hourly joys be still upon you!   108
            Juno sings her blessings on you.
[CERES]   Earth's increase, foison plenty,   110
            Barns and garners never empty,
            Vines with clust'ring bunches growing,
            Plants with goodly burden bowing;
            Spring come to you at the farthest
            In the very end of harvest.
            Scarcity and wants shall shun you,
            Ceres' blessing so is on you.

FERDINAND
    This is a most majestic vision, and
    Harmonious charmingly. May I be bold
    To think these spirits?   120
PROSPERO   Spirits, which by mine art
    I have from their confines called to enact
    My present fancies.
FERDINAND   Let me live here ever!
    So rare a wondered father and a wise   123
    Makes this place Paradise.
        Juno and Ceres whisper, and send Iris on employment.
PROSPERO   Sweet now, silence!
    Juno and Ceres whisper seriously.
    There's something else to do. Hush and be mute,
    Or else our spell is marred.

IRIS
    You nymphs, called Naiads, of the windring brooks,   128
    With your sedged crowns and ever-harmless looks,   129
    Leave your crisp channels, and on this green land   130
    Answer your summons; Juno does command.
    Come, temperate nymphs, and help to celebrate
    A contract of true love: be not too late.

---

108 *still* constantly   110 *foison* abundance   123 *wondered* wonderful   128
windring winding and wandering   129 *sedged crowns* crowns of sedge (a
river plant)   130 *crisp* rippling

Enter certain Nymphs.
You sunburned sicklemen, of August weary,
Come hither from the furrow and be merry.
Make holiday: your rye-straw hats put on,
And these fresh nymphs encounter every one
138 In country footing.
        Enter certain Reapers, properly habited. They join
        with the Nymphs in a graceful dance; towards the end
        whereof Prospero starts suddenly and speaks; after
        which, to a strange, hollow, and confused noise, they
        heavily vanish.
PROSPERO   *[Aside]*
    I had forgot that foul conspiracy
140 Of the beast Caliban and his confederates
    Against my life: the minute of their plot
142 Is almost come.
        [To the Spirits] Well done! Avoid! No more!
FERDINAND
    This is strange. Your father's in some passion
    That works him strongly.
MIRANDA   Never till this day
    Saw I him touched with anger so distempered.
PROSPERO
146 You do look, my son, in a movèd sort,
    As if you were dismayed: be cheerful, sir.
148 Our revels now are ended. These our actors,
    As I foretold you, were all spirits and
150 Are melted into air, into thin air;
151 And, like the baseless fabric of this vision,
    The cloud-capped tow'rs, the gorgeous palaces,
    The solemn temples, the great globe itself,
154 Yea, all which it inherit, shall dissolve,
    And, like this insubstantial pageant faded,

---

138 s.d. *after which . . . vanish* (i.e., following l. 142)   142 *Avoid* be off
146 *moved sort* troubled state   148 *revels* entertainments (also the dance of
masquers and spectators together at the end of a court masque)   151 *baseless*
fabric insubstantial, nonmaterial structure   154 *it inherit* possess it

Leave not a rack behind. We are such stuff   156
As dreams are made on, and our little life   157
Is rounded with a sleep. Sir, I am vexed.
Bear with my weakness: my old brain is troubled.
Be not disturbed with my infirmity.   160
If you be pleased, retire into my cell
And there repose. A turn or two I'll walk
To still my beating mind.
FERDINAND, MIRANDA   We wish you peace.
                    Exit [Ferdinand with Miranda].

PROSPERO
Come with a thought! I thank thee, Ariel. Come.   164
    [Enter Ariel.]

ARIEL
Thy thoughts I cleave to. What's thy pleasure?
PROSPERO   Spirit,
We must prepare to meet with Caliban.

ARIEL
Ay, my commander: when I presented Ceres,   167
I thought to have told thee of it, but I feared
Lest I might anger thee.

PROSPERO
Say again, where didst thou leave these varlets?   170

ARIEL
I told you sir, they were red-hot with drinking;
So full of valor that they smote the air
For breathing in their faces, beat the ground
For kissing of their feet; yet always bending
Towards their project. Then I beat my tabor;
At which like unbacked colts they pricked their ears,   176
Advanced their eyelids, lifted up their noses   177
As they smelt music. So I charmed their ears
That calflike they my lowing followed through

---

156 *rack* wisp of cloud   157 *on* of   164 (*I thank thee* could be directed to
Ferdinand and Miranda as they leave, rather than to Ariel before he arrives;
the punctuation in F is ambiguous)   167 *presented* acted the part of (?), introduced (?)   170 *varlets* ruffians   176 *unbacked* unbroken   177 *Advanced*
lifted up

180 Toothed briers, sharp furzes, pricking gorse, and
     thorns,
     Which entered their frail shins. At last I left them
182 I' th' filthy mantled pool beyond your cell,
     There dancing up to th' chins, that the foul lake
     O'erstunk their feet.

PROSPERO   This was well done, my bird.
     Thy shape invisible retain thou still.
     The trumpery in my house, go bring it hither
187 For stale to catch these thieves.

ARIEL   I go, I go.   *Exit.*

PROSPERO
     A devil, a born devil, on whose nature
     Nurture can never stick: on whom my pains,
190 Humanely taken, all, all lost, quite lost!
     And as with age his body uglier grows,
192 So his mind cankers. I will plague them all,
193 Even to roaring.
          Enter Ariel, loaden with glistering apparel, etc.
                    Come, hang them on this line.
          *[Prospero and Ariel remain, invisible.] Enter Caliban,
          Stephano, and Trinculo, all wet.*

CALIBAN
     Pray you tread softly, that the blind mole may not
     Hear a foot fall. We now are near his cell.

STEPHANO   Monster, your fairy, which you say is a harm-
197 less fairy, has done little better than played the Jack
     with us.

TRINCULO   Monster, I do smell all horse piss, at which
200 my nose is in great indignation.

STEPHANO   So is mine. Do you hear, monster? If I
     should take a displeasure against you, look you —

TRINCULO   Thou wert but a lost monster.

CALIBAN
     Good my lord, give me thy favor still.

---

182 *mantled* scummed   **187** *stale* decoy   **192** *cankers* festers   **193** *line* lime
or linden tree (probably not a clothesline)   **197** *Jack* knave

Be patient, for the prize I'll bring thee to
Shall hoodwink this mischance. Therefore speak softly.   206
All's hushed as midnight yet.

TRINCULO   Ay, but to lose our bottles in the pool!

STEPHANO   There is not only disgrace and dishonor in
that, monster, but an infinite loss.   210

TRINCULO   That's more to me than my wetting. Yet this
is your harmless fairy, monster.

STEPHANO   I will fetch off my bottle, though I be o'er
ears for my labor.

CALIBAN
Prithee, my king, be quiet. Seest thou here?
This is the mouth o' th' cell. No noise, and enter.
Do that good mischief which may make this island
Thine own forever, and I, thy Caliban,
For aye thy footlicker.

STEPHANO   Give me thy hand. I do begin to have bloody   220
thoughts.

TRINCULO   O King Stephano! O peer! O worthy   222
Stephano, look what a wardrobe here is for thee!

CALIBAN
Let it alone, thou fool! It is but trash.

TRINCULO   O, ho, monster! We know what belongs to a
frippery. O King Stephano!   226

STEPHANO   Put off that gown, Trinculo: by this hand, I'll
have that gown!

TRINCULO   Thy grace shall have it.

CALIBAN
The dropsy drown this fool! What do you mean   230
To dote thus on such luggage? Let't alone,   231
And do the murder first. If he awake,
From toe to crown he'll fill our skins with pinches,
Make us strange stuff.

_____

206 _hoodwink_ cover over   **222** _peer_ (referring to the song "King Stephen was
a worthy peer," quoted in _Othello_ II.3)   **226** _frippery_ old-clothes shop   **230**
dropsy (disease in which fluid accumulates excessively in the body, hence an
insatiable thirst)   **231** _luggage_ junk

235 STEPHANO Be you quiet, monster. Mistress line, is not
      this my jerkin? *[Takes it down.]* Now is the jerkin under
      the line. Now, jerkin, you are like to lose your hair and
      prove a bald jerkin.

239 TRINCULO Do, do! We steal by line and level, an't like
240   your grace.

      STEPHANO I thank thee for that jest. Here's a garment
      for't. Wit shall not go unrewarded while I am king of
      this country. "Steal by line and level" is an excellent
244   pass of pate. There's another garment for't.

245 TRINCULO Monster, come put some lime upon your fin-
      gers, and away with the rest.

      CALIBAN
      I will have none on't. We shall lose our time
248   And all be turned to barnacles, or to apes
      With foreheads villainous low.

250 STEPHANO Monster, lay to your fingers: help to bear this
      away where my hogshead of wine is, or I'll turn you out
      of my kingdom. Go to, carry this.

      TRINCULO And this.

      STEPHANO Ay, and this.
          *A noise of hunters heard. Enter divers Spirits in shape
          of dogs and hounds, hunting them about, Prospero and
          Ariel setting them on.*

      PROSPERO Hey, Mountain, hey!

      ARIEL Silver! there it goes, Silver!

      PROSPERO
      Fury, Fury! There, Tyrant, there! Hark, hark!
          [Caliban, Stephano, and Trinculo are driven out.]
      Go, charge my goblins that they grind their joints
259   With dry convulsions, shorten up their sinews

---

235 ff. (the jokes are probably obscene, but their point is lost; sailors crossing
the *line*, or equator, proverbially lost their hair from scurvy, but baldness
caused by syphilis may be alluded to)   239 *by line and level* according to rule
(with pun on "line"); *an't like* if it please   244 *pass of pate* sally of wit   245
lime birdlime (sticky, hence appropriate for stealing)   248 *barnacles* geese or
shellfish   250 *lay to* apply   259 *dry* (resulting from deficiency of "humors,"
or bodily liquids)

With agèd cramps, and more pinch-spotted make 260
them
Than pard or cat o' mountain.   261
ARIEL   Hark, they roar!
PROSPERO
Let them be hunted soundly. At this hour
Lies at my mercy all mine enemies.
Shortly shall all my labors end, and thou
Shalt have the air at freedom. For a little,
Follow, and do me service.   *Exeunt.*

                           *

❧ **V.1** *Enter Prospero in his magic robes, and Ariel.*

PROSPERO
Now does my project gather to a head.
My charms crack not, my spirits obey, and time   2
Goes upright with his carriage. How's the day?
ARIEL
On the sixth hour, at which time, my lord,
You said our work should cease.
PROSPERO   I did say so
When first I raised the tempest. Say, my spirit,
How fares the king and's followers?
ARIEL   Confined together
In the same fashion as you gave in charge,
Just as you left them – all prisoners, sir,
In the line grove which weather-fends your cell.   10
They cannot budge till your release. The king,   11
His brother, and yours abide all three distracted,
And the remainder mourning over them,
Brimful of sorrow and dismay; but chiefly
Him that you termed, sir, the good old Lord Gonzalo.

---

260 *agèd* i.e., such as old people have   **261** *pard or cat o' mountain* (both
refer to the leopard or catamount)
   V.1 2–3 *time . . . carriage* time walks upright because his burden is light
10 *line grove* grove of lime trees; *weather-fends* protects from the weather   **11**
till your release until you release them

His tears runs down his beard like winter's drops
From eaves of reeds. Your charm so strongly works 'em,
That if you now beheld them, your affections
Would become tender.

PROSPERO   Dost thou think so, spirit?

ARIEL
Mine would, sir, were I human.

PROSPERO   And mine shall.
Hast thou, which art but air, a touch, a feeling
Of their afflictions, and shall not myself,
One of their kind, that relish all as sharply
Passion as they, be kindlier moved than thou art?
Though with their high wrongs I am struck to th' quick,
Yet with my nobler reason 'gainst my fury
Do I take part. The rarer action is
In virtue than in vengeance. They being penitent,
The sole drift of my purpose doth extend
Not a frown further. Go, release them, Ariel.
My charms I'll break, their senses I'll restore,
And they shall be themselves.

ARIEL   I'll fetch them, sir.   *Exit.*

PROSPERO
Ye elves of hills, brooks, standing lakes, and groves,
And ye that on the sands with printless foot
Do chase the ebbing Neptune, and do fly him
When he comes back; you demi-puppets that
By moonshine do the green sour ringlets make,
Whereof the ewe not bites; and you whose pastime
Is to make midnight mushrumps, that rejoice
To hear the solemn curfew; by whose aid
(Weak masters though ye be) I have bedimmed
The noontide sun, called forth the mutinous winds,
And 'twixt the green sea and the azured vault

---

17 *eaves of reeds* i.e., a thatched roof 23 *relish* feel; *all* quite 36 *demi-puppets* tiny dolls (i.e., fairies) 37 *ringlets* fairy rings in grass 39 *midnight mushrumps* mushrooms that appear in the night 41 *masters* forces

Set roaring war; to the dread rattling thunder
Have I given fire and rifted Jove's stout oak   45
With his own bolt; the strong-based promontory
Have I made shake and by the spurs plucked up   47
The pine and cedar; graves at my command
Have waked their sleepers, oped, and let 'em forth
By my so potent art. But this rough magic   50
I here abjure; and when I have required   51
Some heavenly music (which even now I do)
To work mine end upon their senses that   53
This airy charm is for, I'll break my staff,
Bury it certain fathoms in the earth,
And deeper than did ever plummet sound
I'll drown my book.   57
    Solemn music.
    Here enters Ariel before; then Alonso, with a frantic
    gesture, attended by Gonzalo; Sebastian and Antonio
    in like manner, attended by Adrian and Francisco.
    They all enter the circle which Prospero had made,
    and there stand charmed; which Prospero observing,
    speaks.

A solemn air, and the best comforter   58
To an unsettled fancy, cure thy brains,
Now useless, boiled within thy skull! There stand,   60
For you are spell-stopped.
Holy Gonzalo, honorable man,
Mine eyes, ev'n sociable to the show of thine,   63
Fall fellowly drops. The charm dissolves apace;   64
And as the morning steals upon the night,
Melting the darkness, so their rising senses
Begin to chase the ignorant fumes that mantle
Their clearer reason. O good Gonzalo,

---

45 *rifted* split   47 *spurs* roots   51 *required* asked for   53 *their senses that* the
senses of those whom   57 s.d. *had made* (presumably during the previous
speech)   58 *and* i.e., which is   63 *sociable* sympathetic; *show* sight   64 *Fall*
let fall

My true preserver, and a loyal sir
70   To him thou follow'st, I will pay thy graces
Home both in word and deed. Most cruelly
Didst thou, Alonso, use me and my daughter.
Thy brother was a furtherer in the act.
Thou art pinched for't now, Sebastian. Flesh and blood,
You, brother mine, that entertained ambition,
76   Expelled remorse and nature; who, with Sebastian
(Whose inward pinches therefore are most strong),
Would here have killed your king, I do forgive thee,
Unnatural though thou art. Their understanding
80   Begins to swell, and the approaching tide
Will shortly fill the reasonable shore,
That now lies foul and muddy. Not one of them
That yet looks on me or would know me. Ariel,
Fetch me the hat and rapier in my cell.
85   I will discase me, and myself present
86   As I was sometime Milan. Quickly, spirit!
Thou shalt ere long be free.

                    [Exit Ariel and returns immediately.]
            Ariel sings and helps to attire him [as Duke of Milan].

ARIEL
                    Where the bee sucks, there suck I;
                    In a cowslip's bell I lie;
90   There I couch when owls do cry.
                    On the bat's back I do fly
92   After summer merrily.
            Merrily, merrily shall I live now
            Under the blossom that hangs on the bough.

PROSPERO
            Why, that's my dainty Ariel! I shall miss thee,
            But yet thou shalt have freedom; so, so, so.
            To the king's ship, invisible as thou art!
            There shalt thou find the mariners asleep
            Under the hatches. The master and the boatswain

---

70 *graces* favors   **76** *remorse* pity; *nature* natural feeling   **85** *discase* undress
86 *sometime Milan* when I was Duke of Milan   **92** *After* pursuing

Being awake, enforce them to this place,   *100*
And presently, I prithee.   *101*

ARIEL

I drink the air before me, and return   *102*
Or ere your pulse twice beat.   *Exit.*

GONZALO

All torment, trouble, wonder, and amazement
Inhabits here. Some heavenly power guide us
Out of this fearful country!

PROSPERO   Behold, sir king,
The wrongèd Duke of Milan, Prospero.
For more assurance that a living prince
Does now speak to thee, I embrace thy body,
And to thee and thy company I bid   *110*
A hearty welcome.

ALONSO   Whe'r thou be'st he or no,
Or some enchanted trifle to abuse me,   *112*
As late I have been, I not know. Thy pulse
Beats, as of flesh and blood; and, since I saw thee,
Th' affliction of my mind amends, with which,
I fear, a madness held me. This must crave   *116*
(An if this be at all) a most strange story.   *117*
Thy dukedom I resign and do entreat
Thou pardon me my wrongs. But how should Prospero
Be living and be here?   *120*

PROSPERO   First, noble friend,
Let me embrace thine age, whose honor cannot
Be measured or confined.

GONZALO   Whether this be
Or be not, I'll not swear.

PROSPERO   You do yet taste
Some subtleties o' th' isle, that will not let you   *124*
Believe things certain. Welcome, my friends all.

---

101 *presently* right away   **102** *drink the air* i.e., consume space   **112** *trifle*
trick; *abuse* deceive   **116** *crave* require   **117** *An if . . . all* if this is really hap-
pening   **124** *subtleties* (1) illusions, (2) elaborate pastries representing allegorical figures, used in banquets and pageants

[Aside to Sebastian and Antonio]
But you, my brace of lords, were I so minded,
127 I here could pluck his highness' frown upon you,
128 And justify you traitors. At this time
I will tell no tales.

SEBASTIAN *[Aside]*   The devil speaks in him.
PROSPERO   No.
130 For you, most wicked sir, whom to call brother
Would even infect my mouth, I do forgive
Thy rankest fault – all of them; and require
My dukedom of thee, which perforce I know
Thou must restore.

ALONSO   If thou beest Prospero,
Give us particulars of thy preservation;
How thou hast met us here, who three hours since
Were wracked upon this shore; where I have lost
(How sharp the point of this remembrance is!)
139 My dear son Ferdinand.

PROSPERO   I am woe for't, sir.
ALONSO
140 Irreparable is the loss, and patience
Says it is past her cure.

PROSPERO   I rather think
You have not sought her help, of whose soft grace
For the like loss I have her sovereign aid
And rest myself content.

ALONSO   You the like loss?
PROSPERO
145 As great to me as late; and, supportable
146 To make the dear loss, have I means much weaker
Than you may call to comfort you; for I
Have lost my daughter.

ALONSO   A daughter?
O heavens, that they were living both in Naples,
150 The king and queen there! That they were, I wish

---

127 *pluck* pull down 128 *justify* prove 139 *woe* sorry 145 *late* recent
146 *dear* grievous

Myself were mudded in that oozy bed
Where my son lies. When did you lose your daughter?
PROSPERO
In this last tempest. I perceive these lords
At this encounter do so much admire   154
That they devour their reason, and scarce think
Their eyes do offices of truth, their words   156
Are natural breath. But, howsoev'r you have
Been justled from your senses, know for certain
That I am Prospero, and that very duke
Which was thrust forth of Milan, who most strangely   160
Upon this shore, where you were wracked, was landed
To be the lord on't. No more yet of this;
For 'tis a chronicle of day by day,
Not a relation for a breakfast, nor
Befitting this first meeting. Welcome, sir;
This cell's my court. Here have I few attendants,
And subjects none abroad. Pray you look in.   167
My dukedom since you have given me again,
I will requite you with as good a thing,
At least bring forth a wonder to content ye   170
As much as me my dukedom.   171

> *Here Prospero discovers Ferdinand and Miranda*
> *playing at chess.*

MIRANDA
Sweet lord, you play me false.
FERDINAND   No, my dearest love,
I would not for the world.
MIRANDA
Yes, for a score of kingdoms you should wrangle,   174
And I would call it fair play.
ALONSO   If this prove
A vision of the island, one dear son
Shall I twice lose.

---

154 *admire* wonder   156 *do offices* perform services   167 *abroad* elsewhere
171 s.d. *discovers* discloses (probably by pulling aside a curtain across one of
the doors to the stage)   174 *wrangle* contend for

SEBASTIAN   A most high miracle!

FERDINAND
> Though the seas threaten, they are merciful.
> I have cursed them without cause.
> *[Kneels.]*   •

ALONSO   Now all the blessings
180   Of a glad father compass thee about!
> Arise, and say how thou cam'st here. *[Ferdinand rises.]*

MIRANDA   O, wonder!
> How many goodly creatures are there here!
> How beauteous mankind is! O brave new world
> That has such people in't!

PROSPERO   'Tis new to thee.

ALONSO
> What is this maid with whom thou wast at play?
186   Your eld'st acquaintance cannot be three hours.
> Is she the goddess that hath severed us
> And brought us thus together?

FERDINAND   Sir, she is mortal;
> But by immortal providence she's mine.
190   I chose her when I could not ask my father
> For his advice, nor thought I had one. She
> Is daughter to this famous Duke of Milan,
> Of whom so often I have heard renown
> But never saw before; of whom I have
> Received a second life; and second father
> This lady makes him to me.

ALONSO   I am hers.
> But, O, how oddly will it sound that I
> Must ask my child forgiveness!

PROSPERO   There, sir, stop.
> Let us not burden our remembrance with
200   A heaviness that's gone.

GONZALO   I have inly wept,
> Or should have spoke ere this. Look down, you gods,
> And on this couple drop a blessèd crown!

---

186 *eld'st* i.e., longest period of   200 *heaviness* grief

For it is you that have chalked forth the way
Which brought us hither.
ALONSO   I say amen, Gonzalo.
GONZALO
Was Milan thrust from Milan that his issue
Should become kings of Naples? O, rejoice
Beyond a common joy, and set it down
With gold on lasting pillars: in one voyage
Did Claribel her husband find at Tunis,
And Ferdinand her brother found a wife   210
Where he himself was lost; Prospero his dukedom
In a poor isle; and all of us ourselves
When no man was his own.
ALONSO   *[To Ferdinand and Miranda]*
                              Give me your hands.
Let grief and sorrow still embrace his heart   214
That doth not wish you joy.
GONZALO   Be it so! Amen!
    Enter Ariel, with the Master and Boatswain amazedly
    following.
O, look, sir, look, sir, here is more of us!
I prophesied, if a gallows were on land,
This fellow could not drown. *[To Boatswain]* Now,
    blasphemy,
That swear'st grace o'erboard, not an oath on shore?   219
Hast thou no mouth by land? What is the news?   220
BOATSWAIN
The best news is that we have safely found
Our king and company; the next, our ship,
Which, but three glasses since, we gave out split,
Is tight and yare and bravely rigged as when   224
We first put out to sea.
ARIEL   *[Aside to Prospero]* Sir, all this service
Have I done since I went.   226
PROSPERO   *[Aside to Ariel]*   My tricksy spirit!

----

214 *still* forever 219 *swear'st . . . o'erboard* drives grace from the ship by
swearing 224 *yare* shipshape 226 *tricksy* playful, ingenious

ALONSO
> These are not natural events; they strengthen
> From strange to stranger. Say, how came you hither?

BOATSWAIN
> If I did think, sir, I were well awake,
230 I'd strive to tell you. We were dead of sleep
> And (how we know not) all clapped under hatches;
232 Where, but even now, with strange and several noises
> Of roaring, shrieking, howling, jingling chains,
234 And moe diversity of sounds, all horrible,
> We were awaked; straightway at liberty;
236 Where we, in all our trim, freshly beheld
> Our royal, good, and gallant ship, our master
238 Cap'ring to eye her. On a trice, so please you,
> Even in a dream, were we divided from them
240 And were brought moping hither.

ARIEL   *[Aside to Prospero]*   Was't well done?

PROSPERO   *[Aside to Ariel]*
> Bravely, my diligence. Thou shalt be free.

ALONSO
> This is as strange a maze as e'er men trod,
> And there is in this business more than nature
244 Was ever conduct of. Some oracle
> Must rectify our knowledge.

PROSPERO   Sir, my liege,
246 Do not infest your mind with beating on
> The strangeness of this business: at picked leisure,
248 Which shall be shortly, single I'll resolve you
249 (Which to you shall seem probable) of every
250 These happened accidents; till when, be cheerful
> And think of each thing well.

>   *[Aside to Ariel]*   Come hither, spirit.

---

232 *several* various   234 *moe* more   236 *trim* garments; *freshly beheld* beheld our ship equally fresh   238 *Cap'ring* dancing for joy; *eye* see; *On a trice*
in an instant   240 *moping* in a daze   244 *conduct* conductor   246 *infest*
trouble   248 *single* privately; *resolve* explain   249 *every* every one of   250
accidents incidents

Set Caliban and his companions free.
Untie the spell.　　　　　　　　　　　*[Exit Ariel.]*
　　[To Alonso]　How fares my gracious sir?
There are yet missing of your company
Some few odd lads that you remember not.
　　Enter Ariel, driving in Caliban, Stephano, and
　　Trinculo, in their stolen apparel.

STEPHANO　Every man shift for all the rest, and let no
man take care for himself; for all is but fortune. Coragio, bully-monster, coragio!　　　　　　　　　　　258

TRINCULO　If these be true spies which I wear in my head, 259
here's a goodly sight.　　　　　　　　　　　　　260

CALIBAN
　O Setebos, these be brave spirits indeed!
　How fine my master is! I am afraid
　He will chastise me.

SEBASTIAN　　　　　　Ha, ha!
　What things are these, my Lord Antonio?
　Will money buy 'em?

ANTONIO　　　　　　Very like. One of them
　Is a plain fish and no doubt marketable.

PROSPERO
　Mark but the badges of these men, my lords,　　　267
　Then say if they be true. This misshapen knave,　268
　His mother was a witch, and one so strong
　That could control the moon, make flows and ebbs,　270
　And deal in her command without her power.　　271
　These three have robbed me, and this demi-devil
　(For he's a bastard one) had plotted with them
　To take my life. Two of these fellows you
　Must know and own; this thing of darkness I　　275
　Acknowledge mine.

CALIBAN　　　　　　I shall be pinched to death.

---

258 *bully* (a term of endearment)　**259** *spies* eyes　**267** *badges of these men*
signs of these servants　**268** *true* honest　**271** *her* i.e., the moon's; *without*
beyond　**275** *own* acknowledge to be yours

ALONSO
   Is not this Stephano, my drunken butler?

SEBASTIAN
   He is drunk now: where had he wine?

ALONSO
279   And Trinculo is reeling ripe: where should they
280   Find this grand liquor that hath gilded 'em?
   How cam'st thou in this pickle?

282 TRINCULO   I have been in such a pickle, since I saw you
   last, that I fear me will never out of my bones. I shall
   not fear flyblowing.

SEBASTIAN   Why, how now, Stephano?

286 STEPHANO   O, touch me not! I am not Stephano, but a
   cramp.

PROSPERO   You'd be king o' the isle, sirrah?

289 STEPHANO   I should have been a sore one then.

ALONSO
290   This is a strange thing as e'er I looked on.

PROSPERO
   He is as disproportioned in his manners
   As in his shape. Go, sirrah, to my cell;
   Take with you your companions. As you look
   To have my pardon, trim it handsomely.

CALIBAN
   Ay, that I will; and I'll be wise hereafter,
   And seek for grace. What a thrice-double ass
   Was I to take this drunkard for a god
   And worship this dull fool!

PROSPERO   Go to! Away!

ALONSO
   Hence, and bestow your luggage where you found it.

300 SEBASTIAN   Or stole it rather.
         [Exeunt Caliban, Stephano, and Trinculo.]

---

279 *reeling ripe* ready to reel   **282** *pickle* (1) predicament, (2) preservative
(from the horse pond; hence insects will let him alone)   **286** *Stephano* (this
name is said to be a slang Neapolitan term for "stomach")   **289** *sore* (1) inept,
(2) aching

PROSPERO
    Sir, I invite your highness and your train
    To my poor cell, where you shall take your rest
    For this one night; which, part of it, I'll waste   303
    With such discourse as, I not doubt, shall make it
    Go quick away – the story of my life,
    And the particular accidents gone by
    Since I came to this isle; and in the morn
    I'll bring you to your ship, and so to Naples,
    Where I have hope to see the nuptial
    Of these our dear-beloved solemnizèd;   310
    And thence retire me to my Milan, where
    Every third thought shall be my grave.
ALONSO   I long
    To hear the story of your life, which must
    Take the ear strangely.   314
PROSPERO   I'll deliver all;
    And promise you calm seas, auspicious gales,
    And sail so expeditious that shall catch   316
    Your royal fleet far off. – My Ariel, chick,
    That is thy charge. Then to the elements
    Be free, and fare thou well! – Please you draw near.   319
                Exeunt [all except Prospero].

∾ Epilogue

   Spoken by Prospero.

    Now my charms are all o'erthrown,
    And what strength I have's mine own,
    Which is most faint. Now 'tis true
    I must be here confined by you,
    Or sent to Naples. Let me not,

---

303 *waste* spend   310 *solemnizèd* (accent second syllable)   314 *Take* capti-
vate; *deliver* tell   316 *sail* sailing   319 *draw near* come in

Since I have my dukedom got
And pardoned the deceiver, dwell
In this bare island by your spell;
9   But release me from my bands
10 With the help of your good hands.
Gentle breath of yours my sails
Must fill, or else my project fails,
13 Which was to please. Now I want
Spirits to enforce, art to enchant;
And my ending is despair
Unless I be relieved by prayer,
Which pierces so that it assaults
Mercy itself and frees all faults.
As you from crimes would pardoned be,
20 Let your indulgence set me free.   *Exit.*

Epi. 9 *bands* bonds   **10** *hands* i.e., applause to break the spell   **13** *want* lack